NARRATIVES of CONVERSION TO ISLAM

Female Perspectives

Professor Yasir Suleiman

Project Leader and Founding Director
Prince Alwaleed Bin Talal Centre of Islamic Studies,
University of Cambridge

in Association with
The New Muslims Project, Markfield

CONTENTS

Participants — *iv*
Preface — *1*
Executive Summary — *9*

1.	Outline of the project	**17**
2.	Limitations of the report	**18**
3.	Objectives of the report	**19**
4.	A note on terminology	**21**
5.	The participants	**22**
6.	The findings: general comments	**23**
7.	Non-Muslim Perceptions of Islam	**24**
8.	Family responses	**25**
9.	Appearing as a Muslim	**31**
10.	Marriage	**38**
11.	Sexuality	**48**
12.	Domestic violence	**53**
13.	Polygyny	**55**
14.	Divorced women	**59**
15.	Converts' children	**60**
16.	Homosexuality	**64**
17.	Trans-sexualism	**67**
18.	Gender	**69**
19.	Becoming part of wider Muslim communities	**73**
20.	Identity	**80**
21.	Media	**84**
22.	Citizenship, political identity and engagement	**90**
23.	Women's rights	**95**
24.	Guidance and spirituality	**96**
25.	Sufism	**99**
26.	Imams and scholars	**100**
27.	Struggles within the faith	**101**
28.	Concluding Remarks	**110**
29.	Recommendations	**113**

Appendices — *116*
Endnotes — *124*

PARTICIPANTS

Professor Yasir Suleiman
Chair and Project Leader
Batool Al-Toma
Co-Chair
Shahla Suleiman
Project Manager
Ruqaiyah Hibell
Secretariat
Catherine Aganoglu
Kristiane Backer
Alicia Blatiak
Salima Blundell
Jameela Boardman
Karima Brooke
Jameelah Campbell
Myriam Francoise-Cerrah
Andrea Chishti
Marion Cobban
Ann Coxon
Merryl Wyn Davies
Sumayah Ebsworth
Megh Falter
Valerie Gihani
Olga Gora
An Van Ho
Catherine Heseltine

Candace Hoffman-Hussain
Sarah Joseph
Rose Kelly
Laura Zahra McDonald
Joanne McEwan
Fatima Martin
Debbie Miller
Anita Nayyar
Mariam Ramzy
Francesca Reeder
Kathleen Roche-Nagy
Imelda Ryan
Natasha Sadra
Adeela Shabazz
Julie Siddiqi
Aisha Siddiqua
Zahra Sobeiroj
Ioni Sullivan
Yasmin Sullivan
Anisa Temel
Rianne C Ten Veen
Doris Teutsch
Erica Timoney
Mohini Verma
Suaad Walker
Fatima Zohra

PREFACE

As this report will set out, conversion is a complex phenomenon: it implies continuity and change, association and, at times, involuntary dissociation. It looks back, and it looks forward in a journey with meanings which vary with time and from person to person. Female conversion to Islam in particular challenges the binaries of tradition versus modernity and faith versus secularism, by combining in the person of the convert – and her body – both the insider and the outsider, and doing so in a way that has the capacity to dilute the rough and ready distinction between 'us' and 'them'. In the person and body of the female convert to Islam, the 'twain shall and do meet'. For this reason, conversion to Islam presents one of the best empirical domains through which we can explore some of the most entrenched dichotomies involving Islam and Western modernity. Conversion may in fact be as much about Islam itself, as it is about some interpretations of Western modernity to which conversion often poses many questions.

The in-betweenness of female converts poses challenges to our mental and social taxonomies, being insiders/outsiders and intimate strangers at one and the same time, to both the non-Muslim majority and the Muslim minority in Britain. In-betweenness may be a liberating place for the female convert, but it certainly is a hugely challenging one. The question female converts often face is this: 'why would a liberated/free Western woman embrace a backward faith that oppresses her?' This question carries the implication that there must be something 'wrong' with, or 'perverse' about, the female convert to want to do this 'wrong/perverse' thing. The fact that conversion to Islam may be a rational choice made to deal with some real philosophical and existential problems facing female converts in the modern world appears to be an embargoed idea, whether by routine habits of thought, through social acculturation or out of Islamophobic prejudice.

Conversion is often full of joy and pain for the convert and her family and friends, regardless of the faith to which she converts, but no more so than when the faith concerned is a maligned Islam and its followers. For this reason, the Narratives of Conversion to Islam symposia that I had the honour of chairing for this report (as the only male member of the project) were unequalled as an exercise in baring the soul, displaying human vulnerabilities, voicing doubt, expressing unwavering certainty, affirming and re-affirming commitment, revelling in diversity, and lovingly celebrating and braiding the common bonds of humanity that, in their diverse inflections, *seem* to divide us. For many, if not all, of the participants the narratives underlying this report were conceived as journeys of discovery that went backward and forward, with many unscheduled stops to take stock, affirm the direction, refuel and move on. The notion of the journey was in fact so strong in these narratives that some participants suggested inscribing it in the title. In the end, the decision was made to stick to a more mundane title which, I hope, still retains the notion of process in what this report talks about: conversion is always in a mode of *becoming* through which a state of *being* subsists as a core.

This report is exclusively about female converts to Islam in Britain, although the converts who took part in the project came from different ethnic, national, faith and no-faith backgrounds that characterise the plurality of British society. Converting to Islam brings challenges to the female convert on many levels. The report deals with these openly and, I hope, sensitively. The challenge of separating faith from culture impacts the convert from the very beginning of her conversion and may last for a considerable time. Converts often turn to members of the heritage Muslim community for information on Islam, moral support and friendship, but they cannot always tell the difference between what is faith-bound and what is culture-bound in the information that they receive, especially at the start of their conversion. This may present the convert with a confusing picture at a time when she is unsure of her faith. It is not that heritage Muslims knowingly set out to confuse the convert, but they may not always be aware of the fine distinctions between faith and culture in their own belief systems. In this context, the attempt to integrate the convert into a heritage Muslim community (there are many such communities) becomes a matter of absorption where she is expected to dilute her pre-conversion cultural practices into the culture of the recipient community; in some cases she is urged to get rid of these practices altogether in order to become a full Muslim. Either way, conversion has a double trajectory in sociological terms: conversion to a new faith and accommodation/'conversion' to a new culture; although the first kind of conversion is the main subject of this report, the interplay between the two processes of conversion is also explored. Because of this double trajectory, it is not surprising that conversion to Islam is associated, for some converts at least, with culture shock and culture stress, which may or may not colour their views of the conversion experience.

One of the first challenges facing a female convert to Islam is that of dress etiquette. The report deals with this at some length from different angles. The participants expressed a great variety of views on this issue, which has been complicated by the emblematising of the *hijab*, both by Muslims and non-Muslims, as a sign of Islamic identity in a world that is dominated by all kinds of anti-Islamic/Muslim feelings. Some converts see the *hijab* in this way, as a badge of identity, but others do not. Some wear the *hijab* from day one of their conversion, while others do not. Some in this latter group may not wear the *hijab* except when it is required to discharge their religious duties and on other occasions. Others may wear it on and off as they see fit, reflecting their mood, locality[1] or the ebbing and flowing of their religiosity. Some may wear it sparingly, showing strands of hair, but others would use it to cover their hair completely. But regardless of who wears the *hijab* and when, the point is made in the report that there is a distinction to be made between *wearing* the *hijab* and *being worn* by it.

This is an extremely powerful distinction: wearing the *hijab*, rather than being worn by it, puts the convert woman in control. The *hijab*, according to this, is not a matter of display of identity nor is it a veil or a barrier. The female convert wearing the *hijab* in this spirit sets out to dilute its public visibility through engaged action that enables others, Muslim and non-Muslim, to go past it to issues of substance and shared interest that are common to all: those of doing good in the world. For converts of this persuasion, especially, the *hijab* signals modesty (this is the purpose of it anyway), but it is not intended to hide beauty: being modest is not the same thing as being 'frumpy'. And the obsession with it on all sides is considered to be unhealthy because it directs people's attention onto appearances, while in fact the *hijab* precisely aims to downgrade the heightened attention paid to appearances. In addition, the undue attention paid to the *hijab* takes away from the inner journey, silent and invisible, on which every female convert embarks. It is this inner journey and the fulfilment it brings, rather than its outward expression via the *hijab* that sustains the female convert through the ups and downs of her experience. The promotion of the *hijab* as a ubiquitous symbol of identity, by both Muslims and non-Muslims, stands as a barrier against the inner spirituality which female converts would rather highlight as the greatest reward of their conversion. Female converts would definitely prefer to have their conversion read from the *inside out* rather than from the *outside in*. They have not come into Islam to affect change to their appearances, but to develop an inner state of being that requires discipline and demands a radical realignment of personal priorities.

In Western societies where it may be easier for women to wear less than wear more, the *hijab* may look anachronistic in the extreme. On wearing the *hijab* as a convert, a White woman loses the prestige her 'Whiteness' bestows on her, becoming symbolically Black and culturally 'other'. And if she is of a British background, she is made to feel 'non-British'.[2] A middle-class British woman who converts to Islam may, additionally, risk losing her social class, dropping down a notch or two on the social scale, regardless of whether she wears the *hijab* or not. A White female convert may even lose her career, especially if she is in work that puts her in the public eye, as in fact happened to some members of the project. This is why conversion to Islam by White women takes great courage to effect and to display in the public sphere: the loss of social status and/or class can have an enormous cost for the convert and her family. From a different angle, this observation about social prestige may help explain why the conversion of Asian and Black women to Islam, while still equally courageous for other potent reasons, goes unnoticed among the non-Muslim White majority: Black converts lack the social prestige White female converts have, and they are already culturally 'other'.

This 'racial' construction of conversion is replicated among heritage Muslims, but in an entirely different way. The operative concepts here are those of the 'trophy' and the 'mantle-piece'. White female converts report that their conversion is treated as a 'victory' by heritage Muslims, something which they resent because it values them for the 'colour of their skin' rather than for their standing as Muslims: Islam does not attach any value to skin colour or ethnicity, a fact which many female converts find extremely attractive about the faith. When cases of this kind are true, a White convert is seen as a *trophy* and she is figuratively given pride of place on the *mantle-piece* of the Muslim household.

This, it is reported, is not the case with non-White converts to Islam. African-Caribbean female converts report that they are not seen as trophies by heritage Muslims, and there is, therefore, no place for them on the mantle-piece. Here we have a blatant example of the clash of culture with faith among (some) members of the heritage Muslim community. The silent conversions of African-Caribbean female converts do, as a result, go unnoticed and they are made to remain invisible as if they were socially unworthy.[3] This has major consequences for these female converts in psychological terms, as well as for their ability to secure the help and support that they need from heritage Muslims along their challenging journey into and through Islam. As Chair of the symposia and Project Leader, I found this part of the conversion narratives the hardest to bear, although I was buoyed by the resilience of these female converts, the generosity of their spirits, their good humour and their 'staying power'. If female converts wanted cultural reasons to leave Islam, African-Caribbean women would have reasons aplenty to do so. But most do not because they are able to cut through culture to faith.

This report deals with a host of other issues, including marriage, divorce, polygyny, sexuality, domestic violence, mosque provisions for female converts, the challenges facing the children of convert mothers and the role converts may/can play as bridges between heritage Muslims and non-Muslims in society. The treatment of these issues, although necessarily brief in this report, is not monolithic. Muslims, heritage or convert, are sometimes accused of fabricating unity to counter the adversity of their hemmed-in situation in society, but when they are not being attacked on this level they tend to be accused of factionalism, sectarianism or lack of coherence: they are, in effect, 'damned if they do and damned if they don't'. This report may not escape this evaluative syndrome. Our two Centre reports *Contextualising Islam in Britain: Exploratory Perspectives* (2009) and *Contextualising Islam in Britain II* (2012) both met with a similar response, for exactly the same reason, by non-Muslims and Muslims. When Muslims display their diversities, or when they express perfectly Islamic views that are not stereotypical, some non-Muslims may (and do) accuse them of dissembling. By the same token, some Muslims may consider them to be renegades. The idea that 'Islam is not for the faint-hearted' should, therefore, be proffered as one of the first messages to give to any female considering converting to Islam. On this the participants were of one mind.

Like heritage Muslims, converts speak in diverse voices about different issues that affect them as a community/group. Nomenclature is one such arena where different views are expressed. Some converts wish to be called reverts,[4] but others do not. Some may not object to being called New Muslims, but others strongly oppose this nomenclature.[5] The majority do not mind being called converts, but some would rather be called Muslims without any qualification. The best, I think, we can do is to use these names interchangeably, but to be aware of the sensitivities that surround them.

Perhaps a principle of offending less than offending more should be the guiding principle.

Convert women may find their heritage-Muslim husbands wanting as worthy partners, and prefer divorce as a solution to their problems. But often they find that their commitment to Islam may in fact have been strengthened as a result of this parting of marital ways which often sweeps out the detritus of mere culture from the path of an evolving faith journey. As one participant in the project put it: 'This is a case of ditching the man and keeping Islam.' The commitment of these women to Islam is, therefore, real and long-lasting: it is not contingent on being married to a Muslim, although marriage may have been their route into the faith. Conversion may, therefore, be mixed with personal disappointment in the converts' life stories, but never about disappointment with the faith.

Whether a woman converts to Islam through marriage, or for some other reason, no one route into the faith is considered to be more worthy than the others. All the routes to Islam are considered to be equally worthy: there was unanimous agreement among the participants on this issue. The report speculates on why female converts may leave Islam, in spite of the small number of those who in fact do so, but does not offer any definitive views on this because of the lack of information: hard as she had tried to plug this lacuna, the Project Manager was unable to secure the necessary participation from those who had decided to exit Islam. The participants treated this and all of the above issues with openness and an abiding sense of fairness and integrity. There was not a trace of self-pity or apologia in the symposia, but a readiness to tackle difficult issues head on. The fact that some non-Muslims may be maliciously critical of Muslims (including converts) and Islam in no way justifies a defensive and introverted approach to addressing the issues that these female converts are facing. On this there was total unanimity among the participants. 'Islam is not for the faint-hearted' I can hear them now say.

The use of 'narratives' in the title of this report highlights the notions of biography, life-story and the role that memory plays in framing them. In story-telling, memory acts in selective ways and is not always beholden to 'factual' truths, although it may set out to capture and narrate truths of this kind. Story-telling does not have to unfold chronologically: in its normal mode, it combines both psychological time and linear time. It meanders and it flows in a straight line, two qualities that are in evidence in the way this report unfolds. And story-telling recounts events and the impact of those events on the narrator as much as it does offer description, reflection and analysis. What we get is *faction*, a combination of fact and fiction, but only if fiction is understood as retrospective construction. A different group of female converts may, in fact, have produced a set of narratives that differ greatly or ever so slightly from the ones offered here. The reader is asked to bear these reflections on narration in mind in approaching this report.

This report is a summary of the views of the participants, whose names are given at the start of this report, and not a verbatim record of their life-stories or views. This Preface glosses these views and puts broad-brush interpretations on them which are entirely mine (some members of the project may in fact disagree with these interpretations). The project was conducted under Chatham House rules. A complete audio-visual record of the proceedings was produced, to be used exclusively in writing this report. It must, however, be pointed out that the views expressed in this report cannot be associated with any one participant, the Project Leader and Chair, the co-Chair or the Project Manager. To generate consensus, a draft of the report was circulated to the steering group, following extensive revisions for content, accuracy, style, tone and impact. The Project Leader and Chair worked through the comments he received to prepare a new draft. This new draft was sent out to the whole group. The report was subjected to further revisions by the Project Leader and Chair before a new draft was sent to a copy-editor whose comments were used to produce the tenth and final version. With the exception of one member who attended half a day of the project symposia, all members consented to have their names included in the report. It must, however, be pointed out that not every participant attended all the symposia or agrees with every point in the report, but that they all accept its findings as a fair summary of the discussions in which they had participated.

This report was initiated by the Project Leader and financially sponsored by the Centre of Islamic Studies at the University of Cambridge. It is envisaged as the first phase of a project on conversion to Islam in Britain. The next phase will focus on male converts. As Project Leader, I would like to thank Batool Altoma of the New Muslims Project, Markfield for acting as co-Chair and for her help and support in many ways. One of the outcomes of this project is an abiding friendship between Batool and the Centre of Islamic Studies. Shahla Suleiman acted as the Project Manager, and she discharged her duties with (her signature) understated efficiency, unrelenting determination, attention to detail and warm welcome which ensured that the participants felt at ease to pursue their discussions in an atmosphere of trust and friendship. Ruqaiyah Hibbell compiled the first draft of the report, which underwent extensive revisions, and she continued to offer her valuable help by commenting on the two versions that the Project Leader circulated to the Steering Group and, then, to the entire membership of the project. I am grateful to Ruqaiyah for the work she has done, and for doing it with grace and loving commitment. Shiraz Khan stepped in with her usual dedication to design and typeset the report. For that I warmly thank her. Finally, I am happy to acknowledge the support given to the project by the staff of the Møller Centre, Cambridge who ensured we had the best venue to help us work hard and 'eat hard' – very, very hard.

Yasir Suleiman
Centre of Islamic Studies, Cambridge
1 February 2013

EXECUTIVE SUMMARY

1. This report endeavours to describe the experience of women converts to Islam in contemporary British society. The relationship between the convert, the heritage Muslim communities and wider society is explored with reference to their political, social and religious contexts. The convert experience emerges as variously characterised by acceptance and rejection, inclusion and exclusion, integration and isolation. Therefore, conversion is explored here as part of a multi-faceted experience that comprises a complex range of variables which may indeed at times appear mutually contradictory. This is in fact an inevitable result of the existence of contradictory forces and attitudes which the convert to Islam is forced to negotiate.

2. Furthermore, the female Western-born convert often finds herself unwillingly located at the nexus of a 'clash of civilisations' in a social and political context where relations between Islam and the West are too often framed in polarised and confrontational ways. This report attempts to allow the multiplicity of these experiences to be voiced without imposing a 'coherent' (and therefore reductive) narrative on them or forcing these narratives to speak for artificially constructed 'sides' in the (arguably illogical) 'West versus Islam' debate.

3. Converts and the Muslim communities they become embedded in are not homogenous groups: they reflect the diversity of cultures, ethnicities, expressions of faith and socio-economic realities that characterise Britain. The needs of converts also reflect this diversity, which necessitates the development of respectful responses mindful of these multifarious characteristics.

4. This report outlines the importance of establishing a British-orientated perspective on Islam. Despite the existence of converts as early as the 1800s (if not before), it is only post 9/11 that an embryonic British Islamic identity has been emerging and may appear more pronounced amongst the children of converts. Notably here, identity is perceived as both authentically British and authentically Islamic. History has demonstrated that as Islam has spread across cultures and continents, new Muslims of diverse ethnicities have felt entitled to retain their

indigenous cultural practices and norms while they have adopted the faith, cultural practices and beliefs intrinsic to Islam. The assimilating formations of Islamic identities have provided a core set of beliefs and practices common to the Muslim world's diverse ethnic populations, providing unity within diversity and diversity within unity.

5. For many converts identity is a fluid and continuous process of self-evaluation and re-evaluation, aligned with the possibility of arriving at a comfortable sense of Self. Generally, conversion entails not so much of the relinquishment of a previous identity but more of a widening of that identity. While acknowledging that they have become part of a minority group in Britain, and are in some senses a minority within a minority, many converts to Islam are able to establish a strong sense of Self and comfortably express a shared identity regardless of their social setting. Others possess a more fractured sense of identity that is shaped by the social context in which they operate. Self-perceptions of identity change or evolve as converts develop their own understanding of their faith.

6. Discussions surrounding appearance explored the influence of dress on identity and examined the extent to which dress is bound up with concepts of the Self for a Muslim woman. Adopting forms of Islamic dress as a means of reflecting Islam has consequential social costs in that, while it sets boundaries in terms of recognition and adherence to Islam, it also creates partition in terms of the degree to which the convert achieves acceptance within wider society. The choice to wear certain forms of dress can induce stress and put pressure upon the convert and lead to unwanted scrutiny and judgment. For those (and particularly White) converts who prior to conversion have not experienced issues of acceptance from wider British society, changing their mode of dress can be a means of contributing to an estrangement from wider society, with them frequently becoming assessed as non-White citizens. This can lead to converts being treated as second class citizens in situations where attitudes towards minority groups are prejudicial.

7. The concept of dress as emblematic of piety was for some converts reinforced by adopting the wearing of Islamic clothing. For others, spirituality was enhanced by not revealing any faith allegiance through forms of dress. The choice made by some converts not to adopt any forms of Islamic dress often led to a focus on altruistic expressions of

faith as a means of demonstrating what it means to be a Muslim. Here, converts were keen to be seen as kind, helpful and useful members of a society in which their faith could be demonstrated through their behaviour. These different responses do not stand in antithetical relationship to each other. In both cases, converts feel beholden to embody visibly 'good' characteristics as Muslims, perhaps in part as a conscious or subconscious response to the pervasive atmosphere of negativity surrounding Islam in the West.

8. How converts negotiate familial and personal relationships following conversion is explored as a means of capturing the on-going tension that frequently prevails in the wake of conversion. This report examines through the shared experiences of participants, what conversion can represent to the families and friends of converts. How converts internalise and present their own conversion, including how tensions are addressed and overcome, is considered. Lifestyle changes were largely viewed in a positive light with an emphasis on life being enhanced and sustained through a strong connection to God.

9. Marriage offers a number of key challenges which are intensified for converts who lack familial support systems when selecting potential partners. The problems inherent in finding safe mechanisms through which to generate introductions to potential spouses are discussed, as are the benefits and problems that marriage itself presents to converts. With the majority of converts entering into cross-cultural marriages the impact of culture on marriage is highlighted.

10. Marriage within Islamic paradigms also presents the possibilities of stretching the boundaries of relationships beyond monogamy to include polygyny.[6] The participants discussed their views on plural marriages. Participants' direct experience of plural marriages enhanced the debate by providing real examples of the complexities such marriages involve.

11. Domestic violence and its impact on the lives of Muslim men, women and families are areas that receive little attention in the discussion of Muslim communities in Britain. There is minimal acknowledgement of how the impact of abusive relationships can be amplified for converts to Islam. Here, a lack of family support may hinder the development of exit strategies from such relationships and prolong the time spent enduring

abusive situations. Misguided religious advice may serve to collude with and perpetuate abuse.

12. Divorce within an Islamic context is frequently problematic for female converts who often lack advocates to ensure that it (divorce) can be initiated by women and that their rights to financial provision and to custodial arrangements for their children are protected.

13. The children of converts are discussed in terms of the extent to which converts are able to raise children to be comfortable with an Islamic identity, despite often lacking a network of support from their own heritage community to enhance and develop their faith. How Islamic identity is created and the extent to which children are able to maintain their faith as they achieve adulthood is also discussed. An infrastructure exists to facilitate Islamic education; however, some of those working within religious schools and mosques seem to lack awareness of the breadth and diversity within British Muslim communities.

14. Often, converts' children navigate a more distinctive personalised expression of Islam. Muslim children of convert parents usually grow up with a more nuanced approach to being Muslim, making them more easily able to cross cultural divides. In terms of marriage partners they are not driven to choose from within a particular ethnic group, but are more free to select spouses from the diversity of Muslim cultures.

15. This report provides frank discussion on how aspects of sexuality impact on the conversion experience. As part of this discourse the views of converts on homosexuality are highlighted. Converts saw themselves as being more acquainted with variation in sexuality due to their Western upbringing, whilst being aware of Islamic principles regarding religious rulings around homosexual and heterosexual relations.

16. The relationship of a trans-sexual convert within heritage Muslim communities raises important issues surrounding the acceptance of difference within these communities. Here, the participants responded with a sense of concern and inclusion, seeking to find an equitable way of allowing transsexuals to find a place within Muslim communities according to the gender they had selected.

17. In terms of maintaining faith, converts detailed how they retain their faith in adversity and the extent to which doubts impinge upon and affect their perceptions of Islam. How Islam is understood and incorporated into their lives as part of a seemingly lifelong project was considered. Converts discussed how they assess theological presentations of Islam and how they form and internalise interpretations of these.

18. Spirituality is at the heart of the participants' relationships with Islam. For many, this took the form of interest in or the practice of Sufi teachings. For others, an intense personal relationship with God took precedence over 'esoteric' practices. Spirituality and the acknowledgement of the oneness of God was the sustaining element for converts in maintaining their practice of Islam.

19. Converts' engagement with heritage Muslim communities provides continual challenges in terms of acceptance and integration. This report explores how converts negotiate and straddle the divides between their communities of origin and their adopted communities, each providing conflicting cultural norms that have to be prioritised. There are dangers of polarised perceptions emerging between converts and wider society or converts and heritage Muslim communities. It was felt that steps need to be taken to prevent dichotomised perspectives of 'them and us' from emerging.

20. In terms of political participation converts are part of a political system that can appear to compromise religious values. Islamic values are sometimes perceived to be incompatible with some values that are considered inherently European. Many converts attempt to develop the skills to bridge these political and religious divides. Conversion to Islam does appear to affect the political outlook of converts. Those who possessed minimal political awareness prior to conversion often became awakened to issues that had been affecting Muslims in Britain and other parts of the world.

21. Lobbying through engagement with Islamic organisations or single issue pressure groups may appeal more directly to those converts who are able to articulate and influence political perspectives that reflect Islamic ideals which are not considered, by many Muslims, to be different from the ideas of the non-Muslim majority in society. There are unresolved

perplexities regarding the extent to which converts have a moral responsibility to take on the 'concerns' of heritage Muslim communities or to respond in a humane way to cultural issues that do not directly affect them.

22. Converts frequently possess an acute awareness of how Muslims are perceived by the wider non-Muslim society. Educated converts can distinguish between Islamic ideals and the everyday practice of many Muslims. As such they have the ability to perhaps present a more balanced view of both Islam and of Muslims themselves that may be more acceptable to the non-Muslim majority in British society. This ability, whilst not always recognised by the majority of Muslims, has the potential to create bridges between the non-Muslim and Muslim elements of British society.

23. Active involvement by converts in mainstream political parties raises issues of acceptance. This involves concerns of how electable a convert would be as a potential candidate for public office, i.e. how would their conversion be perceived by the electorate on either side of the cultural divide? In terms of involvement in existing heritage Muslim political organisations and structures there are particular issues of gaining acceptance, including finding structures not dominated by the tribal or ethnic politics of the ancestral homelands of heritage Muslims. Given their perceptions of the many potential barriers to participation, converts tend to be hesitant to engage in politics.

24. For both heritage Muslims and converts alike, the politically-charged Prevent[7] agenda has proven to be difficult political territory to negotiate. While Prevent programmes have provided some benefits to Muslim organisations and communities, associated counter-terrorism programmes were seen by many participants to have wreaked harm on Muslims across the UK. On the other hand, some participants argued that although the community felt 'persecution through the Prevent agenda' due to the lack of consideration for the nuances of the community, nevertheless they have secured advantages through government actions which have supported their rights. Lack of Muslim-generated initiatives to address the contemporary needs of Muslims in Britain has meant that in order to secure the rights of Muslims, community activists have had to be reliant on both the Prevent agenda and having to resort

to British non-Muslim organisations to fight their battles. Within this vacuum of Muslim-led initiative, the participants recognised that the government has 'set out to engineer its own brand of moderate or co-opted Islam,' thereby attempting to determine the parameters of acceptable Islamic beliefs.

25. Converts saw themselves as part of the global community of Muslims (the *umma*). The concept of the *umma* denotes a compassionate response to the needs of other people. While there was evidence of this collective body of Muslims supporting and aiding those who require help, converts were nonetheless scathing of its applicability when it came to assessing their own needs. Converts were called upon to provide support and help for a variety of international causes but complained that frequently heritage Muslims fail to recognise converts as authentic Muslims. Critically, it was considered that the concept of the *umma* is politicised and idolized and at times used as an escape clause to disengage from politics in Britain and/or to focus on political concerns abroad. The preoccupation with the *umma* was also perceived to remove the need to be self-critical of what is happening in the UK. Too frequently, the concept of the *umma* was applied to demarcate exclusivity and to establish boundaries between Muslims and non-Muslims, which appeared contrary to the spirit of Islam. In terms of the wider Muslim communities, participants disagreed over the composition and nature of the term '*umma*', and the extent to which it did or did not provide for a self-sustaining and supportive Muslim community in contemporary Britain.

26. Women's rights are a highly charged political issue within Muslim communities. While participants were not unanimously supportive of the concept of feminism as commonly defined in the West, the need to raise the status of women within Muslim communities was fully acknowledged. While the Islamic ideals underpinning women's rights receive accolades and applause from heritage Muslims and actually attract many converts to the faith, attempting to realise the practice of those rights has proven more difficult to achieve. Participants were especially critical of the concept of *Sharia* Council/courts operating in Britain in terms of the courts' potential to jeopardise the rights of women.

27. Media interest in conversion has varied from fascinated interest to distorted portrayals of individual conversions. Converts serve to confound and challenge negative racist or stereotypical narratives depicted in the media of heritage Muslims because their culture and heritage is intrinsically reflective of British culture. The small percentage of converts engaged in terrorist-related activity makes headline news. The demonization of Muslims in the mainstream media is a recent (post-1960's) phenomenon. The discourse used to describe Muslims includes a range of pejorative terms. Participants discussed a widely-held belief that two-thirds of non-Muslims derive their information about Muslims largely or solely from the media.

28. The relationship between converts to Islam and the media has seen the media focus largely on converts as a stereotypical group of White, middle class well-educated women. This has led to the exclusion of converts from other ethnicities and socio-economic groups. For example, little coverage has been accorded to conversions within UK prisons or those among other ethnic groups such as African-Caribbean converts, who are thought to be the largest ethnic group of converts to Islam within Britain. Media narratives of conversion as a rejection of Western values, and of Islam as inherently dangerous, form a backdrop of prejudicial discourses through which converts and their families confront largely negative coverage of Islam. From such experiences arise the need to counteract and dispel adverse stereotypes and media coverage. A desire to respond constructively to media representations of converts can be hindered by a lack of knowledge as how to generate effective responses.

29. The consistent theme flowing through the report is the need for increased levels of support for the convert community, formulated as a set of recommendations at the end of the report. Support network organisations need to be openly inclusive and reflective of the multi-cultural composition of Britain's convert population. This necessitates supportive organisations operating at both the local and national levels to lobby for improved provision of services, along with access to decision-making forums, in order to provide responses focused on a range of sources of help and support for converts. These services are required to address the unique issues and concerns facing converts themselves. This does not equate with a desire to establish enclaves of converts but to facilitate their participation with both heritage Muslim

organisations and wider society. Converts have the potential to play a role as bridge-builders between the heritage Muslim communities and British society but they need active and sustainable support in order to fulfil that role confidently.

1. Outline of the project

1.1 The three symposia convened for the *Narratives of Conversion to Islam in Britain* project sought to examine issues faced by female converts to Islam. The symposia provided a forum for reflection on aspects of conversion and enabled articulation of how the participants viewed the effects of conversion on themselves and their family and friends. The meetings took place in Cambridge, England over three weekends set at intervals from October 2011 to January 2012.

1.2 This was a unique forum, the first of its kind to be held in the UK. Participants were able to discuss the issues they have faced in a safe and frank forum, and many insights emerged to inform future debates, discussions and ideas about what it means to be a female convert to Islam in contemporary Britain.

1.3 It is anticipated that the project will be extended to include the narratives of male converts to Islam, on whom little systematic research has been conducted in the UK.

1.4 The forum was initiated by Professor Yasir Suleiman, the Founding Director of the Prince Alwaleed bin Talal Centre of Islamic Studies at the University of Cambridge, in association with Batool Al-Toma of the New Muslims Project at the Islamic Foundation in Markfield, Leicestershire. The project was organised and managed by Shahla Suleiman.

1.5 Preparing for the symposia involved an initial brain-storming meeting of a small steering group consisting of the organisers along with five female converts from various parts of the UK. This meeting was followed by a one-day discussion forum to confirm the relevant issues relating to conversion and to consider which of these warranted further investigation. Sixteen female converts from a diversity of ethnic and social backgrounds from across the UK participated in this one-day discussion to further develop the initiative.

1.6 The discussions were based on the awareness that there is scope to augment the contemporary material being generated through different projects about British converts. This led to the choice of a discursive exploration of the array of issues facing converts to Islam thus allowing the emergence of deeper insights.

1.7 The three symposia were designed to produce a report to inform British society as a whole, particularly the British heritage Muslim community, the convert community and the wider non-Muslim British society about the issues pertinent to conversion as well as the varied nature of life for converts to Islam in contemporary Britain. The intent of the report also sought particularly to dispel misapprehensions and misrepresentations of female converts to Islam.

1.8 The structure for each symposium provided a set of questions to guide and direct the discussions (See Appendices). This did not presuppose a direct response to the questions but was a means to delve into the issues that the questions raised. The weekends were divided into three or four discussion forums, each session beginning with a chosen female convert speaker. Speakers presented an overview of their conversion experiences by addressing some of the questions that were outlined for the forum, providing the impetus for all participants to contribute their own personal perspectives and views. The symposia provided a platform for a candid self-probing examination of the issues affecting converts. It was expected that fresh perspectives and insights stemming from a range of different social and cultural frames of reference (provided by the diversity of converts present) would be highlighted, serving to enrich subsequent debates on conversion to Islam. Participants were encouraged to speak freely and openly. The discussions were conducted under Chatham House rules where confidentiality is maintained with respect to who said what during the symposia.

2. Limitations of the Report

2.1 In practice, the discussions were limited by the amount of time that could be accorded to each session, by the interpretations the participants placed on the questions offered and the subsequent dialogues that emerged. Several of the main speakers emphasised certain aspects of the questions, resulting in some potential areas of debate not being addressed. This was inevitable given the wide subject matter and the limitations of time. Certain themes were thoroughly debated by the participants, which meant other issues received less attention. The central focus of the discussion converged on the themes of appearance, marriage and family, as this report makes clear.

3. Objectives of the Report

3.1 Besides providing a platform to elucidate aspects of conversion that have received little or no attention through contemporary literature on conversion to Islam and to add detail to existing research, this report also aims to provide a medium through which the opinions of converts can be expressed. Converts' voices have habitually been filtered out of debates on Islam because they are not considered authentic or authoritative, by either heritage Muslim communities and/or the wider non-Muslim society. The symposia and this report represent an opportunity for this lack of representation to be addressed.

3.2 Converts possess the potential to be a powerful and transformative influence on both the heritage Muslim community and wider British society. Given the talent and high levels of education of many converts it is puzzling why the convert presence remains relatively low-key and subdued within the UK. The living spiritual and ethical values derived from Islam provide converts with the ability to act as conduits for Islam in Britain. Little is understood amongst the general British public about the rich legacy of Islam's historical heritage, the breadth and depth of its ideas, its vision of a fair and just society and its spirituality. Converts have a role to play in disseminating the positive contributions Islam can make to the wider society.

3.3 Historically, prior to the post-1950 mass immigration to Britain of Muslims predominantly from the Indian sub-continent, converts to Islam played a much more dynamic role within British society than that currently exhibited by modern converts. The Victorian convert, Abdullah Quilliam, founder of the Liverpool Muslim Institute, is illustrative of the transformative power of converts within British society. Contemporary examples, albeit of lesser impact, could include the recently deceased Muhammad (pbuh)[8] biographer Martin Lings, and the late Hasan Gai Eaton, the British writer on Islam, as well as the still current charitable fund-raising musician Yusuf Islam.

It could be argued that the mass migration of Muslims into Britain has suppressed the need for, and in some ways the ability of more recent converts to play that more dynamic role. Muslim communities are now able to provide spokespeople often as second, third, or fourth-generation citizens, who can effectively relate to and understand British culture and who are able to act as effective representatives of Islamic interests in Britain.

3.4 It is important to provide a platform for minority views since converts can be considered as a minority group within the wider minority of Muslim communities. Not all converts will necessarily perceive themselves in such terms; some successfully integrate into Muslim heritage communities where the distinction between convert and heritage Muslim becomes blurred or non-existent. But for others the status of being members of a minority persists. Converts who originate from ethnic backgrounds distinct from the White British population may perceive themselves to be part of a community with an exacerbated 'minority within a minority' status. In particular, the voices and experiences of African-Caribbean converts to Islam are largely absent. It is probable that converts from an African-Caribbean heritage form one of (if not) the largest group(s) of converts to Islam in Britain. Little has been documented on converts from this background within the UK and there is also no reliable data available which estimate the number of converts to Islam from this heritage, or the rate at which conversion is occurring. Documenting the personal experiences of African-Caribbean-heritage converts might also serve to highlight contemporary racism prevalent within heritage Muslim communities, which tends to work to exclude and marginalise these converts to a point where their presence is neither welcomed nor acknowledged.

3.5 A similar lack of focus is accorded to non-White converts from non-Christian backgrounds, such as Sikhs and Hindus, who are not physically distinguishable from heritage Muslims of South Asian origin. The extent to which inter-communal prejudice involving Muslims, Sikhs and Hindus continues to afflict members of the latter two groups when they convert to Islam has not been addressed in academic studies on conversion. The ability to physically blend into heritage Muslim communities means that the narratives of this constituency of the convert population attract little outside attention and remain largely unheard. The stories of converts of Chinese extraction are also missing.

4. A note on terminology

4.1 During the symposia converts referred to themselves as 'converts', 'reverts', 'new Muslims' and 'those who had embraced Islam'. There is no appropriate term in the English language that conveys the idea that a person has decided to embrace Islam. The Arabic verb *aslama* conveys the concept of peaceful submission. In Arabic usage, people adopting the Islamic faith may be understood to *enter* (*yadkhul*) or *embrace* (*ya'taniq*) Islam. Since the advent of Islam no value has been attached to the point in a person's life at which he or she make a conscious decision to acknowledge their awakening to the faith. The first Muslims were known for their devotion to Islam and Prophet Muhammad, and the idea that they, or indeed he, have somehow converted or reverted to Islam did not exist. Through personal submission to God, people were considered to have entered the fold of Islam.

4.2 For the purposes of clarity the term 'convert' is used throughout this report to convey the concept of moving to Islam from another faith, or from no faith. Other terms such as 'New Muslim' have not been used because many of the subjects of this report have been practising Muslims for many years and would not, therefore, now consider themselves as new to Islam. The term 'New Muslim' can confer freshness and vitality, though some converts view it as a pejorative term. 'New Muslim' can signal an implied lack of acceptance and lack of knowledge about Islam, or of being a poor representative of Islam.4.3 The Oxford English Dictionary defines the verb 'convert' as 'to turn in position or direction', 'to turn one's attention', or 'to undergo a change of character, nature, form or function', from the classical Latin ***convert re***, 'to turn about, turn in character or nature, transform, translate'.[9] As a noun, 'convert' is 'a person converted to, or brought to embrace and profess any religious faith or doctrine'.[10] The term 'convert', therefore, denotes that one has made a conscious decision to embrace a way of life which is in some way fundamentally different to previous beliefs and practices. An alternative to the verb 'convert' is 'revert' which means 'to become conscious again, to regain one's senses', or 'to recover, to improve in condition'.[11] The term 'revert' is favoured by some because it is considered to reflect a returning to the natural state of *fitra* (an Arabic concept which denotes a pure and God-given state of being, reflective of the human soul's natural status as submissive to God) which is imprinted upon every individual at birth.

5. The participants

5.1 The symposia comprised forty-nine participants including the Project Leader (the only male) and the Organiser, who are both heritage Muslims. Some of the participants attended all three of the symposia whereas others only attended one or two. Several participants attended for one day only. A wide age range was present, from early twenties to seventies. The ethnic composition of the symposia was mixed. It included African-Caribbean heritage converts, Asian heritage converts and mixed heritage converts from a variety of backgrounds. The remainder of the participants consisted of White Europeans, predominantly British, and a small number of White Americans. The group was largely composed of educated women. The majority were graduates, many holding master's degrees and several holding doctorates. It would have been desirable to have representations from a wider spectrum, but this was not possible. The participants were all resident in England, Scotland or Wales and they covered different age groups.

5.2 Participants came from a number of previous faith backgrounds, including a mixture of different Christian denominations, Jewish, Sikh, Hindu, Buddhist, agnostic and atheist. Several of the participants had fathers who had converted from the family's faith of origin to different faiths. One participant's father had converted from the Hindu faith to Christianity and another's from Judaism to Christianity. This meant that there was already a history of conversion within their families. This heritage of conversion did not necessarily lessen the difficulties faced by the converts in approaching issues surrounding conversion with their families.

5.3 Some of the participants were recent converts to Islam whilst others had converted some decades previously. What characterised these longer-term converts was that, despite the obstacles that they had encountered during their individual journeys to Islam, they had remained Muslim. It is impossible to predict whether each conversion will last for life but to date the women shared the characteristics of resilience, perseverance and determination stemming from a strong faith in God.

5.4 One limitation of the participant sample was that it was not wholly representative of the female convert population in the UK. This resulted from female converts from other sectors of the convert communities not contacting the organisers to express an interest in taking part in the symposia along with the difficulty of generating wider contacts into the convert community by both the participants themselves and the organisers.

5.5 The participants attending the symposia did not include any representatives from the marginalised populations of female converts who remain on the fringes of Muslim communities or who are invisible for a variety of reasons, for example former prisoners or women who have converted and then left Islam. It should be acknowledged that this latter group is a particularly difficult one to reach let alone to bring to a forum. People who have left Islam or who are no longer practising the faith may not be willing to publicly discuss the reasons. More marginalised groups may feel less comfortable attending an organised discussion.

5.6 In terms of the inclusion of converts from mainstream interpretations of Islam represented in Britain, there were no ultra-conservative (*Salafi*) or *Shia* converts present. Although orthodox conservative tendencies were occasionally apparent within the discussion, the majority of participants presented a more spiritually influenced interpretation of Islam. Where possible, more encouragement is needed at the proposed future symposia for these alternative and different perspectives to be represented. The effect of more dominant voices emerging through the discussions also needs to be taken into account. Where it is apparent that one particular line of thought is being promoted, the opportunity for alternative opinions to emerge needs to be encouraged. Otherwise, a desire for harmony may lead to what social psychologists call, 'group think', where dissenting individual opinions are modified to produce convergence towards the majority view; the point being not to reach group consensus, but to present as many individual voices as possible.

5.7 It was recognised that participants would not necessarily be able to speak to all points or with equal degrees of knowledge or authority. A deeper understanding of issues may be elicited through further future research. A forum of this nature is limited in its ability to deal with gaps in knowledge and it was recognised that these were unavoidable.

6. The Findings: general comments

6.1 Conversion narratives are subject to an on-going and continual process of revision by those who have embraced Islam. As converts develop and change so they may modify their perception of their acts of conversion and their subsequent lives. Portrayals of the processes of conversion are also subject to differing interpretations and changes of emphasis according to the audience to whom these stories are being presented. Social, political and emotional frameworks influence the audience's understanding of what is still often viewed as an aberrant act which requires justification. One participant acknowledged that she had about six different versions of her conversion narrative which were adjusted according to whom she was conversing with.

6.2 Overall, the symposia provided a largely comfortable discussion of often uncomfortable issues. The main themes frequently reiterated in various forms by different participants highlighted the generic issues facing converts across the UK regardless of social class and educational background. Belonging to particular ethnic groups appeared to be a factor which exacerbated some of these issues. The main areas of concern that emerged from the symposia were acceptance and rejection, loneliness and isolation, inclusion and exclusion, identity, marriage and family.

7. Non-Muslim perceptions of Islam as perceived by converts

7.1 During Elizabethan times conversion to Islam was termed 'turning Turk'.[12] Participants felt that this term still reflects the dominant British discourse surrounding race, reflecting ignorance and a lack of knowledge. Islam is perceived variously as a mysterious, sensuous, exotic and barbaric 'Other' to traditional Britishness. Post 9/11 and post 7/7 perceptions of Muslims, as frequently depicted in the mass media and reflected in attitudes held widely by the general British public, have seen the image of Muslims change from that of the 'Other' to the 'dangerous Other'. Muslims are perceived to have influence in wider society disproportionate to their actual minority status within British society. Perceptions exist that Muslims are engaged in insidious plans/schemes designed to impose Islam on Britain and change British culture. Unprecedented monitoring of Muslim communities at all levels of British society, from the government and its attendant security agencies down to primary school teachers, represents both real and perceived features of contemporary life in Britain.

7.2 It is within this atmosphere that new converts to Islam present their newly found faith to frequently bewildered or suspicious families, friends, colleagues and the public, and at a time when their knowledge of the faith may be fairly elementary and they may be experiencing feelings of uncertainty or a lack of self confidence in their ability to defend their decision to convert. Converts are also frequently expected by non-Muslims to become spokespeople for every global event which involves Muslims. Aside from the fact that this expectation is itself unreasonable, unless a convert has extensive knowledge of international politics, this is an expectation which they are often ill-equipped to respond to. Converts may also be expected to be experts on Islam and address and counter any prejudice that is presented to them. If they fail to adequately respond they are then considered to not understand their faith or to be ignorant and unaware of the dangers that emanate from Islam. They are often considered to be naive fools who have been duped.

7.3 The prevalent discourse surrounding what it means to be British and the norms of British behaviour and attitudes seem to be challenged by British converts. The rise in the number of converts throughout the UK will increasingly serve to challenge previously held assumptions about Islam as indigenous Britons convert and seek to apply Islamic ideals in a British context by developing an understanding of Islam that is integral to life in Britain.[13]

8. Family responses

8.1 It is recognised that the responses of converts' families to their conversions can have a profound effect on the psychological well-being of the convert at a time when they are frequently experiencing an array of conflicting thoughts, emotions, uncertainties and apprehensions about the choices they have made and the effect that their decision to convert to Islam may have on their most meaningful relationships.

8.2 It was agreed that during the early post-conversion phases most converts experience isolation and loneliness which are exacerbated by the loss of friends and problems arising within families and social networks. One participant plaintively commented, 'my life is so lonely, my question to God is: Why me?'

8.3 There appeared to be a number of ways in which the participants revealed their change of faith allegiance to their families. Some converts chose to reveal their conversions almost immediately, while others took years to do so. It has been often suggested that the fervour of the new convert makes the revelation of their conversions more difficult than it necessarily needs to be. This can be due to the (often new) convert's intransigence, by insisting on strictly interpreting Islamic principles and demonstrating adherence to their new faith at every opportunity. Often their approaches soften over time, allowing for more accommodation with the behavioural norms of their families. It is here that services providing advice would be valuable to converts, to help them explain their conversion to their families in ways that appear less confrontational.

8.4 Responses by families to conversion are varied and may be affected by geographical settings. For example, it is much easier to go unnoticed as a Muslim in a large city than in a small town or village, where a change in appearance and behaviour may attract comment and where the family may be concerned about unwelcome attention. The psychological environment in which someone lives and interacts can also affect their perception of conversion. For example, if a person has previously experienced a lot of adverse life events, relatively, their conversion to Islam may not be perceived as problematic and may be welcomed for the positive effects it may induce. One participant noted that the mother of one dual heritage young man who had converted remarked, 'I was so relieved he was not into drugs and crime'.[14] In other cases, in families which are characterised by an open acceptance of diversity, conversion may not be contentious.

8.5 The personality of family members is another factor affecting responses. The responses elicited by the converts' families varied and contained a wide spectrum of diverse reactions, from extreme rejection to acceptance.[15] Some of the participants' family members who adhered to strong religious beliefs were more readily able to accept that there were alternative paths to God. An appreciation of God and the divine, therefore, became the point through which family members of different faiths could connect, helping to transcend doctrinal differences. At the other end of the spectrum, some families' strong religiosity provided more problems of acceptance over their conversion. One participant recalled a mother who refused to acknowledge that her daughter was married because she had not married within the Catholic Church. At an even more extreme level, deeply established religious families could react to conversion as an instance of religious betrayal.

8.6 Participants from atheist families found they lacked a frame of reference in common with their family members through which they could share an understanding of the purpose of creation and life. Their conversion was more frequently viewed by their families as a loss of rationality, and the validity of spirituality was not understood or acknowledged.

8.7 It appeared that the participants from families that were atheist and who viewed organised religion as 'nonsense' experienced on-going problems in gaining acceptance for themselves as Muslims from their families, often continuing over many years. There was an overall apparent lack of respect for religious practices. Responses would include ridicule and offensive remarks and attempts to belittle, diminish and undermine the convert's beliefs. One participant cited her atheist mother's alarm that her grandchildren were going to be indoctrinated into Islam and brainwashed into a set of mythical 'fairy like' beliefs, from which they would suffer irreparable harm. Another participant noted that her father's attitudes, fuelled by media misrepresentations of Islam, had grown increasingly hostile to Islam and Muslims, however, his Muslim daughter and her family and friends remained exceptions to such hostility and continued to be welcomed into his home.

8.8 One participant noted how during the early years of her conversion to Islam she felt as if she led a dual existence, with one part of her life as the Muslim convert, and the other as the person she had been prior to conversion. She reported that 'for two years [she] split [her] personality', becoming one person amongst her family and another when she was with Muslims. This was partially due to the unfavourable and extremely critical reception she had received from her mother as well as the extreme awkwardness and unease with which she attempted to reconcile and incorporate her Islamic beliefs into her life. She has now successfully integrated her two lifestyles and describes herself as content with the person she has become.

8.9 One participant's conversion provoked extremely dramatic reactions from her family. The father, unable to accept that his daughter had converted to a 'barbaric and uncivilised' faith, threw her out of the house. Her mother's response was to join a group who viewed the adoption of Islam as being 'brainwashed' into a dangerous cult. The brother responded by joining the British National Party to prevent the further 'Islamification' of Britain, starting with his sister. The family reported to enquiring neighbours that their daughter had died. When the participant travelled abroad to engage in humanitarian work her family informed the security services of the country concerned that their daughter was a terrorist. This family saw the adoption of Islam as descending into an underclass. They felt that their own social status as middle class citizens was threatened. They tried by all possible means to reconvert their daughter to secularism, including trying to imprison her in their house.

8.10 Such hostile reactions reflected the profound disappointment presented by a convert daughter failing to realise her parents' dreams, aspirations and ambitions for her life. Parents can experience a form of bereavement for loss of expectations and hopes which they perceive to reflect negatively on their parenting, their culture and their values. Parents may agonise over the loss of traditional cultural rites of passage. For example, a father may regret the loss of the opportunity for him to walk his daughter down the aisle when she marries, or to attend the baptism of a grandchild.

8.11 Often, a strong sense of failure and guilt prevails where parents of converts consider where they went wrong, and how they could have prevented this religious conversion from happening. They may agonise over what may have been lacking in their own system of beliefs and how they had failed to effectively convey the essence of their beliefs to their children, whether these have a religious or non-religious basis. Conversion may represent an attack on their lifestyle and behaviour, constituting a rejection of the upbringing and socialisation provided by parents. Reactions noted by participants on the part of their families included snobbery and a sense of cultural superiority. Parents often express concern that the prevailing Islamophobia[16] exhibited in society would place the convert in danger, would threaten their employment prospects and prove damaging to their general welfare. Concerns were also conveyed that converts were limiting their choices in life, and denying themselves the simple pleasures taken for granted in British society.

8.12 Participants noted that where adverse responses were received to the conversions at the outset, over time there was a tendency for an accommodation of beliefs to be incorporated into the workings of the family. Often siblings proved more amenable to changing their outlook. The participants thought this might be a reflection of the differences in sibling relationships with the convert, to that of parents, who may feel a greater sense of responsibility towards their children. One participant noted how the relationship with her brother had improved to the extent that he would ensure that there was *halal* food prepared for family meals, although it had taken eight years for him to reach this position.

8.13 Sustaining relationships with family often involved a number of compromises on the part of the convert. One participant described how, although she felt extremely uncomfortable socialising in the presence of people consuming alcohol, she was prepared to do so in order to maintain family relationships. She noted, however, how this would be used against her by her family, who saw her compromises as a form of hypocrisy. This led to the question of why, if she had compromised in one area, she could not compromise in another. Her freedom to set her own boundaries regarding what was permissible behaviour was constantly being challenged by her family's dismissive attitude toward her efforts at improved relations.

8.14 More positively, participants of African-Caribbean heritage noted that family relationships post-conversion were generally less fraught with tensions, and that families tended to be more open and accepting of religious diversity. This was thought to be in part due to a strong spiritual and religious tradition inherent in African-Caribbean culture with a strong belief in God proving to be a common, shared point of reference.

8.15 Many of the participants were aware that the ways in which their parents had raised them were compatible with Islam, and had provided a foundation from which they moved forward to accept Islam. Such parental input could include religious upbringing and teaching, or those moral and ethical values that are recognised in every culture, including mercy, compassion, truthfulness, honesty and justice. In this context the adoption of Islam was viewed not as a rejection of parental values but as an extension of them.

8.16 The effect of difficulties experienced by converts, and the new spiritual context in which these tensions arise, frequently serve to heighten spirituality, which assists converts in facing adversity and when dealing with the on-going issues of life. The participants attested that becoming Muslim was a great gift from God which had enabled them to cope with the difficulties that living as a Muslim in Britain can entail. A strong relationship with God provided spiritual sustenance that enabled the participants to appreciate the blessings in their lives, and to cope with adversity when it arose. Where non-believers may lose hope, and become frustrated and disillusioned when faced with adversity, Muslims may be able to accept the challenges of life as part of the path that God has chosen for them, and may be able to understand that adversity offers benefits by enabling people to develop worthy qualities within themselves. It was recognised that strong faith coupled with trust in God can prevent people from relying on the crutches of alcohol and drugs which are increasingly used as methods of coping with the difficulties of life within the wider society. In this respect, conversion was considered to be extremely liberating.

8.17 For many participants, a myriad of lifestyle changes had been enacted which included: re-evaluating existing friendships; developing alternative friendship groups; considering employment in terms of its compatibility with Islamic beliefs; adapting forms of dress and appearance; changing the way in which interaction with relatives and family occurred; and developing social activities and interests that reflected a preoccupation with spiritual rather than materialistic perspectives on life.

8.18 One participant commented that her lifestyle had not changed so dramatically. Before conversion to Islam, she had been visiting friends' homes getting 'stoned', listening to music and cooking and eating together. Today, she is still visiting her friends, making *dhikr*, and cooking and eating together. She would sit with people who were drinking alcohol if it was important to maintain a relationship with them, as she considers that honouring the ties of kinship and friendship is more important than the order not to sit in the company of somebody consuming alcohol or drugs.

8.19 Attending restaurants that serve non-halal meat and alcohol was considered acceptable by some of the participants, on the basis that it was a means of providing a venue for socialising and strengthening family ties. It was also justified on the basis that it is acceptable in Islam to eat the (non-pork) meat of Jews and the Christians, although how it could be verified that those slaughtering and preparing the meat were in fact Jews or Christians was not considered.

8.20 Accommodation was frequently made for non-Muslim family members, although compromises that involved sitting with relatives who were consuming alcohol left many converts feeling extremely uncomfortable. One of the participants stated that she still attended social occasions such as parties hosted by non-Muslims. Others felt more comfortable in the presence of Muslims than non-Muslims, and avoided pubs, clubs and parties. Some participants felt that it was not easy to know the boundaries of when to engage in certain activities which might compromise their Islamic beliefs. There were issues surrounding socialising in segregated forums. For some, this meant restricting participating in social activities to those that were deemed appropriate by those who promote segregation. For many participants, avenues for seeking acceptable forms of socialising were restricted, and it was considered essential to form networks which enable Muslim women to meet together and enjoy the company of each other. For some, occasions such as Eid and Ramadan – usually characterised by community sharing and celebration – served to emphasise experiences of loneliness, through the notable lack of companionship.

9. Appearing as a Muslim

9.1 Throughout the symposia, a lot of attention was paid to issues surrounding appearance, and, therefore, issues surrounding dress are addressed in this report at some length. This section seeks to address why converts take on particular forms of dress, and how their understanding of Islam is reflected through dress codes. The social costs of presenting oneself outwardly in society as a Muslim were examined, along with an effort to understand how converts counteract the negative reactions which they may encounter. There was an attempt to determine whether there is a relationship between piety and dress.

9.2 Clothing worn by strictly observant women across the Muslim world is thought not to have been affected greatly by the influence of Western-inspired fashion. Styles of clothing tend to reflect the culture and climate of a specific country. The basic commonalities of covering the *awra* (private parts of the body) and of wearing clothing that is loose enough to not display the sexual characteristics of a person, are upheld by practising Muslims throughout the Muslim world.

9.3 Dress can be a powerful symbol signifying the changes that converts experience, as they seek to understand themselves and their identities as Muslim women. This may involve experimentation or the adoption of a variety of forms of dress commonly associated with Muslim women, for example, the headscarf, the *niqab* (full-face veil), the *jilbab* (ankle-long coat-like dress), or the *shalwar-kameez* (tunic with trousers). This may be indicative of a need to conform to their new community. It may signify a preoccupation with symbolism and with the external trappings surrounding religious faith or it may be an attempt to reject perceptions of imposed Western norms of dress. Adopting concepts of modesty may also express a need to convey a spiritual connection through dress. Whilst some participants had adopted traditional dress indigenous to heritage Muslim communities (e.g. the *Abaya* – the long black cloak worn by mostly Arab Muslim women), a common approach amongst the remainder of participants was the adaptation, to varying levels, of Western styles of dress to accommodate Islamic concepts of modesty and decency.

9.4 Presenting oneself as a Muslim, either through forms of dress or by informing people of one's religious faith requires a degree of confidence. It also begs the question of why it is important to converts to be known as Muslim in a largely secular society, where faith allegiance is usually privately discussed and is not usually apparent through appearance. A change in dress is the most visible and obvious change and one which elicits the strongest reactions from non-Muslims. It is described by participants as akin to a rite of passage. It physicalises the boundaries between Muslim and non-Muslim, reinforces a sense of belonging to the Muslim community and makes it easier to be accepted by the latter.[17]

9.5 One participant maintained that she had taken 'a strong stand to wear *hijab*, to declare who I was to other people' through her dress code. For some, the headscarf became what has been termed a 'banner of identity' (Allievi, 2006), while for others it was part of the process of drawing closer to God.[18] Some participants adopted the headscarf on an *ad hoc* basis, wearing it only when they thought it appropriate, and some wearing it only in the presence of other Muslims.

9.6 One participant who had adopted the headscarf asserted that the headscarf was a minor issue, stating that no sanctions were given in the Qur'an for not wearing one. She considered there were far more important issues to be addressed which often fail to be discussed. This led to the question of why so much emphasis is placed upon the way Muslim women present themselves in public, by both non-Muslim commentators and by male and female Muslims, who appear to spend an inordinate amount of time discussing how women should dress. It would appear that this is an attempt by both non-Muslims and Muslims alike to exert control over women by enforcing certain dress codes. Mode of dress is undoubtedly significant, and adhering to a prescribed view of dress may be relevant to acceptance within Muslim communities. For example, within some *Salafi* groups there appears to be pressure or encouragement to adopt the *niqab*. The headscarf can also be a source of tension between modernists, who do not see the need for it, and traditionalists, who maintain that it is requisite to faith. For some, the headscarf is not a problem in itself although the way it is perceived by others may be.

9.7 The adoption of the headscarf may be a precondition for marriage to some Muslim men.[19] The headscarf is intended to divert attention away from the wearer, but in areas where it is not frequently observed it may have the opposite effect. One participant who lives in a small town felt it too conspicuous to wear a headscarf in public, deciding that she was unable to deal with the unwarranted attention that this might attract. Allievi maintains that the decision to wear a headscarf may involve a degree of 'exhibitionism'.[20] This claim was not supported by the discussions in the symposia.

9.8 For some of the participants, the adoption of the headscarf was a visible emblem of a deeper spiritual awakening. It was a means of feeling closer to God, acknowledging the interplay between the inward and the outward, and the effects each has upon the soul.[21] Adopting the headscarf, along with modest dress, was perceived as a liberation and emancipation from the tyrannies of the fashion industry.[22]

9.9 The headscarf and modest dress were viewed as feminist symbols, allowing women to reject representations by society of women primarily as sexual beings. This may signify a refusal to be defined by sexuality, in contrast to the overtly sexualised representation of women which dominates contemporary society. It allows for a rejection of the rampant materialism associated with fashion and with the constant emphasis on discarding 'dated' dress, and the associated waste of resources that this produces. Nonetheless, some participants derived satisfaction in expressing modesty through the wearing of fashionable, yet modest, clothes.

9.10 Those elements within society which are eager to ensure conformity to a sexualised agenda may retaliate by labelling modest forms of dress as 'frumpy' or 'dowdy'. Modestly-dressed women are perceived as failing to make the most of their appearance, by not utilising their physical assets in a society in which women are encouraged to use overt displays of their sexuality as a means of advancement. The right to define the parameters for what is considered 'frumpy', along with the ability to project such views onto others, was strongly rejected by a number of the participants. Prophet Muhammad said, 'Allah is beautiful and loves beauty'. Therefore, Muslims are encouraged to adopt clean and smart appearances and to opt for moderation in all things. The conflation of beauty with sexuality is rejected in Islam. The development of internal beauty is regarded as more valuable than a focus on external appearance.

9.11 The decision to wear a headscarf did not appear to be taken lightly by participants, and was often considered for a number of years before it was adopted. For some participants, the decision to wear a headscarf became important as their faith deepened, and they felt drawn towards wearing it. It was widely acknowledged by the participants that visibly appearing to be a Muslim could lead to forms of stress and pressure. The constant awareness that their behaviour is being scrutinised in terms of an Islamic identity, and of the need to be presenting the best behaviour in all possible circumstances, can become tiring. The discussion of this issue included how the wearing of the headscarf conferred upon a White person, a non-White status. A convert might then be subject to questions regarding their nationality and the country of origin of their parents. The White convert is transformed from 'us' into 'them'. Many White headscarf- or *hijab*-clad converts experienced their first racist attack after becoming Muslim.[23] Wearing a headscarf was considered helpful within the Muslim community, but frequently unhelpful within the broader society, because of its political symbolism. People may assign a political significance to the headscarf in spite of its being worn for its spiritual meaning.

9.12 Prior to adopting the headscarf, one participant described how she had previously viewed *hijabi*-wearing Muslim women as angelic beings, who she could never live up to. It is a commonly held view amongst some Muslims that the headscarf represents a form of protection for women, and that women who wear it are like 'protected pearls'. This participant joked that she had a 'pearl disorder', because she considered that she did not conform to idealised expectations of a Muslim woman. Even the pin that secured the scarf seemed to take on incredible power for her.

9.13 In 1950's and 1960's Britain, it was common to see all manner of women wearing headscarves in public, and it was almost compulsory to wear a headscarf or hat when attending church. As fashions and ideas about dress have changed, the headscarf has become more and more restricted to certain ethnic minorities – peasants, Travellers and older women. It is now uncommon among British women, unless they have a medical condition affecting the hair.[24]

9.14 The headscarf as worn by Muslim women has become associated in the media and accepted by the general public as a form of religious-political assertiveness, a rejection of Western values, or an adoption of the strident symbolism of fundamentalist religious thinking. The wearing of headscarves by women from the Asian sub-continent is more tolerated, in terms of it being a part of their culture. For a White female British convert, wearing a headscarf in an Islamic style may be seen as an aberrant rejection of British cultural values, and evidence that there is something awry, such as eccentricity or weirdness, in the personality of the wearer.

9.15 The mode of wearing the headscarf can also be an important factor whether or not a convert is recognised as a Muslim. Styles of headscarf-wearing vary, and some styles are associated with certain cultures or faith groups. For example, Rastafarian women wear headscarves reflective of West African headscarf styles. Within African-Caribbean cultures, it is common for women to wear headscarves and, therefore, the wearing of a headscarf as a Muslim may prove less of a hurdle to overcome (or simply less of an obvious Muslim signifier) for converts from this heritage than it is for others. One participant with African-Caribbean heritage commented that it was still commonplace to cover the head to attend church. Her adoption of the headscarf had not imposed cultural sanctions on her from her indigenous community, and was not viewed as unusual.

9.16 While some had adopted the headscarf immediately following conversion, other participants experienced an often painful awkwardness due to a protracted period of wishing to wear a headscarf. While a convert may desire to wear a headscarf, they may feel unable to appear in public wearing one, or may feel uncomfortable in public while wearing one. Some participants commented that they had worn a hat, bandana or a scarf tied in a relatively similar style, before graduating to a recognisably Islamic form of headscarf.

9.17 Several participants mentioned reverting to these alternative head coverings at times when they considered wearing the headscarf to be particularly problematic. One participant remarked on wearing a hat, both generally and particularly, when boarding a plane so as not to alarm other passengers who may fear being seated next to a Muslim or harbour concerns about the presence of a potential terrorist in their midst. This participant emphasised the importance of inward, as opposed to outward, expressions of Islam, while others thought such action unnecessary, pandering to the prejudices of non-Muslims.

9.18 The participants found that the anticipation of possible negative reactions to presenting oneself as a Muslim out in wider society, can prove worse than the reality of doing so. One participant described how as a student, after years of deliberating, she finally plucked up the courage to go outside wearing a headscarf. She wondered whether she would be spat at, but instead experienced the anti-climax of no one taking the slightest interest in her appearance. However, she did find the experience of explaining why she was wearing a headscarf to an enquiring lecturer a traumatic one.

The social costs of wearing a headscarf

9.19 It was reported that women experience varying forms of discrimination from wider society if they choose to wear a headscarf in a traditionally Islamic style. Some Muslim converts asserted that it has never posed problems and that there are instances when it has worked to their advantage.[25] One participant recalled first wearing her headscarf to work, and how the attitudes of her male colleagues changed markedly. Her male colleagues became more respectful, would no longer swear or read the erotic "Page 3" in a British tabloid newspaper in front of her and, instead, enquired about her faith. 'This gave them the opportunity to be human beings, rather than reactionary Islamophobes,' she said. Converts set high store by integrating Islam into all aspects of their lives, including their work. However, it is also a sad fact that female converts, whether or not they wear the headscarf, but especially if they do, end up paying a heavy price in their careers. Some participants lost their jobs when it was discovered that they had converted to Islam.

9.20 Dressing in the variety of forms that constitute 'Islamic dress' frequently leads to non-Muslim family, friends, colleagues and the wider society imposing a set of assumptions on the wearer. It is often presumed that converts have adopted a style of dress that reflects a barbaric and oppressive set of beliefs that serve to subjugate women and deny them their free will and freedom, making them less than equal to men. This way of thinking serves to segregate Muslim women from other women. Muslim women are perceived as oppressed, servile and subjugated, while Western non-Muslim women are perceived as the epitome of emancipation. Current is the idea that such forms of dress have been imposed by a patronistic, if not mysogynistic Muslim society, which stamps its cultural authority on the female convert. Converts are even perceived as having become 'Pakistani' or 'Arab.' It is not uncommon for White converts to be subjected to verbal abuse, for example, by being called 'White Pakis.' Conversely, negative perceptions of White female converts, accused of having loose moral values, exist among some members of the heritage Muslim communities who retain a cultural view of them as 'White slags'. The appearance of converts with African-Caribbean heritage frequently goes without notice within heritage Muslim communities where, despite the adoption of forms of 'Islamic dress', these particular converts often remain ignored and invisible.[26]

Choosing not to wear a headscarf in public

9.21 A number of participants had chosen not to wear a headscarf, or had abandoned it after previously wearing it. There has been less interest in female converts who choose not to wear a headscarf and there is, therefore, less commentary available on this subject.[27] While removing the headscarf was perceived by some as providing space in which an intensifying spirituality could flourish, other participants achieved the same spiritual state by wearing the headscarf.

9.22 Some of the participants had made a conscious choice not to wear a headscarf, although they each adopted their own interpretation of modest dress. Several of the participants were working through ideas surrounding the headscarf, and had not arrived at a stage where they had decided for or against it. Some converts who had been Muslim for a number of years and who had previously worn a headscarf, made a conscious decision to abandon it. One participant was worried by the political meanings placed on the headscarf among segments of British society. She commented that wearing a headscarf made her the subject of ready-made stereotypes that she found extremely offensive.

9.23 The headscarf was seen by some as detracting from spirituality. The non-headscarf-wearing converts were conscious of the importance of publicly displaying their faith by exhibiting certain types of behaviour, for example refraining from backbiting, showing generosity, humility or selflessness or helping strangers in need of assistance. Participants who had decided not to wear a headscarf, or who did not feel ready to wear a headscarf in public, were nonetheless aware that it is necessary that their ethical stance is seen to have a connection to their Islamic faith.

9.24 Some participants did not consider the headscarf as a necessary religious obligation and so did not wear it. However, without the visible identifier of a headscarf, it often became difficult to be recognised as a Muslim by other Muslims. Attempts to circumvent this situation were made through the practice of addressing other Muslims with Islamic salutations. This is normally coupled with active attempts to display behaviour in accordance with Islamic norms, in the hope that such behaviour would be recognised as Islamic by non-Muslims. This form of self-presentation was also considered a subtle form of *dawa* (call to Islam) where non-Muslims may be affected by Islamic behaviour, and may be led to enquire or become inquisitive about Islam, without being subject to active proselytising. For these participants, 'subtle *dawa*' was considered more appropriate than wearing a headscarf, perceived as 'obvious *dawa*'.

9.25 Several participants who had yet to reveal their conversions to their families, and who had chosen at present not to adopt a headscarf, shared their desire for public recognition from strangers that they are practising Muslims, but as represented by their behaviour rather than by their dress. However, these same women felt unable to hazard revealing their conversion to the most intimate members of their families and thus gain recognition of their new spiritual state from these key individuals. These converts were waiting for the seemingly elusive 'right time' when they felt prepared and better able to defend their decision to convert to Islam. One participant described the confusion she was experiencing and attributed it to the need to protect her family from the uncertainties she felt over her own understanding of her new faith.

10. Marriage

10.1 The symposia ranged over a variety of issues pertaining to marriage, which included how converts meet prospective partners and the etiquette of arranging marriages in a cross-cultural context. Issues surrounding the lack of sufficient guidance and family support regarding the choice of marriage partners were considered. The need for advice and counselling both pre- and post-marriage was proposed. Aspects of marital breakdown and divorce were explored. Controversies surrounding plural marriages were debated.

10.2 Discussion around marriage focused on the extent to which this social institution had lived up to the expectations of participants, particularly in relation to Islamic ideals, which are frequently cited as one of the factors encouraging women to convert to Islam. According to Islamic belief, marriage is widely considered to constitute half of one's expression of faith, the other half being piety. It was discussed that single convert women in Islam are often viewed with embarrassment by heritage Muslims and that they do not find a niche within the Islamic cultural structure. Discussion also focused on culture, specifically on the problems of addressing different cultural expectations within marriage.

10.3 Common to many of the conversion narratives told by participants was the introduction to Islam through a boyfriend, fiancée or husband. It has been noted that the most frequent route into Islam is through marriage.[28] The orthodox Islamic view is that for a non-Muslim man to marry a Muslim woman he must first convert to Islam,[29] while it is permissible for Muslim men to marry *ahl al-Kitab* (People of the Book, i.e. Jews and Christians). That being the case, many non-Muslim women decide to convert either before or during their marriage to a Muslim husband. This kind of marriage may give rise to what has been described by Kevin Brice as 'conversions of convenience,' where conversion occurs but results in little impact or change upon the behaviour or attitudes of the convert.[30] Brice contrasts this to what he terms 'conversions of conviction,' where converts actively adopt Islam. Many of the participants challenged this as a false dichotomy, having been introduced to Islam through a relationship but nonetheless developing profound and committed 'conversions of conviction'. Indeed, cases were cited where women left the man who had originally 'brought' them to Islam as they found their partner's adherence to the faith too weak. As one participant put it, they 'ditch the man but keep the Islam'.

10.4 Many of the participants had converted to Islam either following marriage or through a romantic involvement with a Muslim man, leading to an active interest and then an induction into the Islamic faith. One participant was reluctant to admit the role that her husband had played in introducing her to Islam, as though it detracted from her own worth as a convert. Most of the participants had been introduced to Islam through some form of personal contact with Muslims. The typical pattern appeared to be a gradual, slow process of movement towards the faith, induced by a growing awareness and understanding of Islamic precepts. Conversion was frequently associated with the experience of living in a Muslim country, where the behaviour of Muslims stirred an interest in Islam. Husbands were not portrayed or seen as pressuring, or even cajoling, but as generally showing a positive representation of Islam through their behaviour and attitudes. Where a romantic involvement had petered out, the introduction to Islam had nevertheless touched the heart of the convert, leading to an awakening and realisation that she wanted to develop a deeper involvement with the faith.[31]

10.5 A number of the participants commented positively on the marriages they enjoyed and the Muslim men they were married to. One participant, who had been married for 44 years and had converted to Islam after 27 years of marriage, stated that she had received nothing but support throughout from her husband. There had been no pressure on her to consider conversion. Prior to this participant's conversion, her husband had shown a great deal of respect for her Christian beliefs, to the extent that he would buy Christmas trees for her while they lived in a predominantly Muslim North African country, encouraging her to celebrate Christian religious and cultural festivals.

10.6 For other participants, the adverse behaviour of Muslim men had proven to be a test of their Islamic faith. While the conversion of some of the participants had occurred via an independent intellectual interest in the faith or spiritual awakening, they had for the most part subsequently married Muslim men, or were now considering the likelihood that they would do so. One participant who had converted as a result of an intellectual journey and a research-based exploration of Islam, was keen to emphasise that the reason for her conversion was not linked to a man. Her interest in Islam had initially been sparked by meeting Muslim Senegalese women and a need to inform herself about Islam in order to refute their beliefs.

10.7 The participants agreed that conversions could not be categorised as 'worthy' or 'unworthy', and that it was inappropriate to attempt to judge the value and validity of a particular route to conversion. It was considered that as God guides people to Islam, relationships and marriages are merely another vehicle for facilitating such guidance.

African-Caribbean converts and marriage

10.8 The ideals of Islam pertaining to marriage provided the African-Caribbean women among the participants with a structure and pattern for marriage which they admired. African-Caribbean women came from a culture characterised by matriarchal structures in which women, predominantly as single-parents, are responsible for providing for the family, and for the decision making within it. For these African-Caribbean women the idea that marriage to a Muslim man would relieve them of that stressful, lonely and exhausting position was appealing. It was noted with much regret that far too frequently African-Caribbean men are not able, for a variety of reasons, to live up to their wives' expectations of what constitutes a good husband. While many male African-Caribbean Muslim converts are able to assume the trappings of Islamic forms of dress and language infused with Islamic salutations, they have proved unable to make the internal changes to their personalities necessary to be a supportive and providing husband, even while they in turn expected women to be obedient and subservient. This frequently meant that following marriage to Muslim African-Caribbean men, African-Caribbean women were in a similar situation to the position they had been in prior to marriage, but with the additional burden of being expected to fulfil the role of an obedient wife. This is a clear example, among many that are found in this report, where Islam and culture don not always converge in Muslim life.

10.9 One participant described tensions between her idealised expectations of marriage and the reality of her own experiences. For women of an African-Caribbean heritage the disappointments of marriage within their own communities, where sources of support often stem from other women rather than men, led them to anticipate more equitable treatment when entering into an Islamic marriage. They had expectations of being cared for by a Muslim man, despite the role of a husband as a sole provider becoming less common. Their expectations of a caring husband, who would provide for them and their children, were rarely realised by Muslim men.

10.10 By way of exemplification, another participant of African-Caribbean heritage commented on how she perceived, in her non-Muslim parents' marriage, a father who was 'very respectful to her mother'. After tolerating for many years a poor marriage to a Muslim of African-Caribbean heritage, she became an unsupported single parent struggling to raise five children on her own. Help was provided by her non-Muslim family and non-Muslim friends. It became difficult to convey a positive image of Islam to her children, who she brought up without any help or assistance from heritage Muslim communities. All but one of her children are now practising Muslims. Her son, who is not a practising Muslim and who is far from impressed with Islam as he has witnessed it, now asks the confounding question of why she is still encouraging women from her African-Caribbean heritage community to become Muslim when this may condemn them to a life as an unsupported single parent. She now finds Muslim women in their early twenties coming to her, suffering from the same plight.

10.11 It was mentioned that with so many Muslim men of African-Caribbean heritage marrying women from other ethnic groups, there is a dwindling pool of potential husbands for African-Caribbean female converts. Their cultural tradition encourages them to choose partners from their own ethnic group because they believe they are less likely to receive proposals of marriage from outside their heritage communities predominantly due to racism.[32] While White converts marry into a wide range of other ethnicities, the tendency amongst female African-Caribbean heritage converts is to marry within their own ethnic groups by choosing male African-Caribbean heritage converts.[33] It is unusual for these women to marry Muslim men from different ethnic backgrounds, although it is not altogether unheard of.

10.12 One participant commented that there was no active community available to assist and strengthen African-Caribbean converts' families. Islam is not a private affair and Muslims are expected to live as part of diverse communities. The Nation of Islam, an African-American Islamic organisation, which incorporates a strong emphasis on Black Nationalism, was considered to be more effective in addressing the impact of racism, oppression and inequality affecting sectors of the African-Caribbean communities, and was, therefore, better placed to serve the needs of African-Caribbean heritage converts to Islam in Britain than any other UK organisation.

10.13 Participants not of African-Caribbean heritage felt unable to engage with the above discourse. The lack of knowledge of issues facing African-

Caribbean converts may again be due to the low profile of these communities, and the lack of interest which is shown toward their well-being by heritage Muslims. These other participants also felt hesitant to offer observations on a community of which one is not part, partly because of a prevailing culture of political correctness which frequently seems to stifle comment. The participants with an African-Caribbean background considered that many African-Caribbean heritage men, who convert to Islam, do so without first addressing personal problems and historical issues and legacies. These can include coming from single-parent families themselves, the lack of suitable role models on which to fashion their behaviour and identity, and dealing with racism and low expectations. Adopting Islam was currently considered within these communities to be fashionable for men, and there is, therefore, a rush to adopt Islam without understanding the responsibilities that it entails.

Finding a suitable husband

10.14 Participants of all ethnicities noted the difficulty of finding suitable marriage partners. For those who were not married, finding a place within existing Muslim communities proved problematic. Not being married could lead to a lonely and often isolated existence because opportunities to socialise and find a place within the Muslim community are easier to access when married.

10.15 One participant commented that following her conversion she had lost all sense of reason. No one was available to help her, she had no external reference points and, therefore, her common sense was not applied and used.[34] This may be characteristic of the early stages of conversion when converts are consumed by idealism and fail to apply their critical faculties to information and ideas that are presented to them. This temporary abandonment of rationality and lack of judgement can have dire consequences for converts considering marriage proposals early on.

10.16 One participant who had married two days after being introduced to her husband questioned the practice of arranged marriages in the context of converts to Islam. Her own difficult experience of marriage illustrated the risks involved. She enquired as to why the heritage Muslim community lacked awareness of the responsibility to safeguard convert women's welfare. There is often haste to persuade converts to get married, often to unsuitable prospective partners such as political refugees or men seeking British passports.[35]

10.17 Many participants were wary of the concept of arranged marriages and of the idea of marrying someone they did not know well. The heritage Muslim community usually has family networks to provide introductions to potential spouses and are able to scrutinise their characters and to assess compatibility.[36] Several had chosen to get to know Muslim men who they had met through their own volition. This was more akin to forms of dating but with an awareness of Islamic etiquette, although time spent together did not involve the use of chaperones. Concerns over arranged introductions had deterred one of the participants from considering remarriage and led her to ask: 'How much change was I prepared to introduce into my life?' As Islamic events were mostly segregated by gender, the opportunities for meeting men were limited, making women rely on friends or the wider Muslim community for introductions, resorting to marriage agencies or personally navigating the potential dangers of meeting a prospective husband through the internet.

10.18 Issues surrounding finding suitable partners for marriage continued across generations. It was noted that finding partners for the children of converts was also beset with problems as most of their extended family are non-Muslim and cannot, therefore, provide recommendations for suitable potential spouses. Both converts and their children can face prejudice from heritage Muslims who may regard them as 'not Muslim enough for marriage'.

10.19 The discussion revealed expectations that converts will meet Muslim men who reflect Islamic ideals in their behaviour and respect the rights of women within marriage. Participants anticipated that the virtuous attributes of Prophet Muhammad would be exemplified in their husband's personalities. Although the financial maintenance of the home and family are the responsibility of the husband within an Islamic marriage, a participant enquired about the extent to which women were expected to compromise their expectations of marriage to conform to the social and economic realities of contemporary life. Many men do not earn enough money to be the sole providers in a household where good standards of living are maintained, and that can often only be achieved and sustained through the contributions of a working wife.

Pitfalls facing converts in marriage

10.20 The Islamic community is the only religious community in Britain which will not refuse to marry couples without a civil marriage first being contracted. One participant raised the possible benefits of altering this system so that an Islamic marriage would not be contracted without a civil marriage having first taken place. This, it was considered, would safeguard the interests of both partners and, in particular, convert women who would have some redress through the British legal system if the marriage was to fail. Several participants advocated that a civil marriage should be insisted upon. It was acknowledged that although a civil marriage does not offer complete protection from abuse, without it 'you would not know if your husband is already married'. Marriages in Muslim countries are legally registered so, as one participant commented, 'if someone in the UK is attempting to opt out of a civil ceremony that would be highly suspicious.'

10.21 It was suggested that converts should ensure that they have a written marriage contract and should not feel hesitant about acquiring one. Some find this a difficult subject to broach because it appears to be offering a legalistic approach to marriage. Pre-nuptial agreements are beginning to be introduced into British culture but are still viewed as the preserve of the wealthy seeking to safeguard a fortune. In British culture a civil marriage contract is compulsory and, therefore, forms part of the decision-making process that couples usually follow when entering into marriage. However, these contracts do not normally specify the rights and obligations of the couples concerned. However, this should not stop a female convert from demanding that the rights and obligations of both partners be inscribed in the Islamic marriage contract.

10.22 The discussion showed that another concept alien to British culture is to marry a person you have met very recently, although converts frequently do this. This demonstrated the need for reputable people to assist converts in their choice of marriage partners and for those who have the ability to scrutinize prospective partners to make an assessment of the suitability of the marriage. Pre-marriage counselling would also assist converts to develop their self-knowledge and awareness when making their choice of partner.

10.23 Participants raised the acceptability of dating Muslim men in order to assess their compatibility before contemplating marriage. It was thought that it was permissible within the bounds of Islamic etiquette if the meetings took place in a public place where the couple were unlikely to be alone together and provided that they both possessed knowledge of what was acceptable behaviour within Islamic strictures. It was considered acceptable, and even desirable, to have an emotional attachment before the marriage had been contracted; it is *zina* (adultery, marital infidelity) that is forbidden and not love. Most of the younger participants seemed determined to get to know a potential partner thoroughly before marriage, and saw love as the correct foundation for marriage.

10.24 Concerns were voiced over the pitfalls that might face both male and female converts through marriages, often arranged by some Imams. Converts can be encouraged to marry quickly and the newest converts are often particularly susceptible to this. When converts do not have the support and protection of their families they are particularly vulnerable. Men and women who wish to secure British passports present themselves on the internet through Muslim marriage websites as potential marriage partners. Older female converts seem particularly vulnerable to the advances of younger men, often seeking financial support along with citizenship. Instances were cited in discussion of converts being encouraged to marry poverty-stricken Muslim men from war-torn countries. These men may be psychologically damaged, without passports and unemployable in their own home countries, where they find themselves considered ineligible for marriage. Issues were raised concerning the *mahr*, (dowry), given to a woman on her marriage and signifying the willingness of the husband to provide and care for his wife. 'Men had been seen pulling the small change out of their pocket', one participant said. These small offerings are not considered appropriate examples of *mahr*. 'This was never the way of Prophet Muhammad'.

10.25 It was thought necessary to encourage Muslim organisations such as the Council of Mosques and the *Sharia* Councils (when they are willing to act) to help prevent the abuse of marriage, in particular by offering support to women seeking marriage. For instance, an Islamic *dawa* Centre is currently involved in assessing prospective marriage partners on application from those seeking marriage.

Conflicting cultural norms in marriage

10.26 The converts participating in this study appeared to be unprepared for the cultural expectations of behaviour within Islamic marriage. There is a marked lack of recognition within the community that converts have their own personal and cultural history which they bring with them into Islam. The convert is perceived to be untainted by other cultural accretions; there is, therefore, a commonly held idea that the convert will automatically shed her culture as if it has been of no value to her. Husbands from a culture different to their convert wives frequently expect that their own cultural norms are to be accepted as part of Islam itself, whereas the culture of the wife was naturally to be discarded. 'You are Muslim; you don't have a culture which is yours!' was how one participant voiced this attitude.

10.27 Participants felt that many badly informed Muslim men consider that by marrying a convert they will be accessing a pure form of Islam. Her culture, they believe, will be Islam. Many of the participants attached considerable value to their indigenous cultures particularly in terms of the foundation it provided when entering Islam. Becoming Muslim is perceived by converts to have been building upon the best aspects of their original culture and values, not a rejection of them.

10.28 One participant was previously married to a heritage Muslim who objected to her singing in the kitchen, on the grounds that other men might hear her voice and become attracted to her and, therefore, he considered singing forbidden in Islam. Other participants found the demands of high domestic standards in the home exhausting to the point that they felt that their own sense of personality and identity was being eroded.

10.29 Acceptance of converts was a key issue for those marrying heritage Muslims, along with how to accommodate themselves within the marriage-family structure. A growing number of mixed marriages between young professionals illustrate that the Muslim community is increasing its acceptance of cross-cultural marriages. Converts also experience doubts regarding the authenticity of their conversion which at times is called into question by both husbands and families, and affecting how well they are received.

10.30 One participant narrated the following story: A heritage Muslim went into the mosque committee room and told those gathered about a new

Muslim convert and was greeted with '*subhana Allah*' and '*Allahu Akbar*'.[37] When he then informed the committee that he intended to marry the same convert he was met with '*astaghfir Allah*'.[38] They told him he was crazy and could not do such a thing. Examples of such attitudes abound. If a convert succeeds in marrying a Muslim from a tightly-knit community, she will not only gain a spouse, but also a whole social network, the acceptance of which may be a prerequisite to her being received as a Muslim by the new family and community.

10.31 It was found that attitudes towards converts within heritage Muslim families vary. One participant found that her mother-in-law, despite being a traditional Pakistani woman who spoke no English, readily accepted her as a spouse for her son on the grounds that she was a Muslim. In contrast, members of the extended family took five years to accommodate the marriage. This participant stated that she had actively sought marriage with a heritage Muslim rather than a convert because she wanted her children to have an extended family who were Muslim.

10.32 One convert who married a Pakistani man had to do so without the presence of her family because *goras* were forbidden to attend the ceremony.[39] The White population is frequently seen as dirty, immoral and *kafir*.[40] When the *gora* becomes Muslim there is confusion, leading to acceptance, but at arms-length. This is coupled with the concern that a White woman will take a man away from his family and culture. One participant detailed how her husband's family were overtly hostile to his plans to marry her because they wanted him to marry his cousin. The repercussions of their subsequent marriage meant that he had to seek assistance from the police to deal with the continued harassment he experienced from members of his extended family, unhappy with his choice to marry a convert. Marrying a non-British Muslim person can also be problematic for the British family of a convert. One participant reported that her family did not have a problem with her conversion but strongly opposed her marriage to a Pakistani.

11. Sexuality

11.1 Little has been written on issues of sexuality in relation to Muslim converts. The focus on sexuality in the symposia, therefore, provided a forum where previously unexplored issues could be openly considered in a way that signposts avenues for future research. It was hoped that this initial discussion might also lead to the development of appropriate mechanisms to address dilemmas for converts stemming from ossified religious rulings.

11.2 One participant felt that 'Islam does not have a problem with sex within the boundaries of marriage'. In many Muslim societies 'sex is alive and well and extremely sensual'. Weddings have traditionally provided a forum for a true celebration of female sexuality. Within Islam, sex is seen as a matter of private intimacy with a spiritual dimension that is extremely important in the mutual development of a married couple. Traditionally, poetry has formed the medium through which the richness of sexuality has been expressed. One participant considered that sexuality expressed only within the bounds of marriage leads to an intensified sexual relationship because the sexual energy is directed towards one person. Prophet Muhammad enjoyed being in the company of women. He was open to discussion about sexual issues and a legacy of expressions of sexual intimacy exists throughout the *hadith*.[41]

11.3 Nevertheless, participants felt that cultural transmissions of ideas about sexual behaviour had distorted an originally straightforward practical Islamic approach to sexuality. Some of the participants stated that this appears to be particularly the case within South Asian Muslim communities in the UK. It was pointed out by participants that converts do not have to accept every interpretation of Islam as defined by communities that have experienced massive cultural dislocation as a result of migration and settlement in the UK. The losses of indigenous cultural safety nets and denigration by and within the host culture have led to introversion and a narrowing of cultural horizons on sexuality.

11.4 Some of the participants felt that the impact of internalising negative sexual attitudes among Muslim communities has led female converts to constrain their natural sexuality, sometimes even to the point of generating frigidity. Altered perceptions of how to behave following conversion may change women's attitudes of acceptable forms of sexual intimacy. One participant considered that the paranoia surrounding sexual behaviour mirrored traditional repressive approaches to sexuality informed by notions of the common cultural dichotomy of the 'virgin versus the whore'. There were concerns that men marrying converts who have internalised such attitudes to sex may find their wives to be like 'prudish statue[s]', no longer able to enjoy an intimate relationship.

11.5 For those female converts who had had previous sexual experiences before contracting a marriage to a heritage Muslim, issues often arise regarding how to deal with the earlier loss of their virginity, and the way that their sexuality may be perceived by their husbands. It was noted that men of heritage background who are attached to the idea of having a 'pure' wife may experience problems with accepting the past sexual experiences that a convert wife may have had. Virginity can also become an issue for the family of the heritage Muslim man, who may question the convert or her potential spouse regarding her sexual history. Issues over virginity may also mask other reasons for parental interference in a potential marriage, relating more to cultural prejudice or racism.

11.6 One participant mentioned the need for men of heritage background to stand up to their families. Some participants felt that issues of virginity should not be pertinent to a prospective husband or his family, who do not have the right to question a potential wife on her behaviour prior to her conversion. They argued that if the family or husband is not content with this response, the convert should not be considering this man as a marriage partner. However, it was pointed out that such issues are not specific to Muslim communities. The same tensions are commonly found within and among other cultures which forbid pre-marital sexual relationships, including the more conservative or orthodox communities of a number of religions.

11.7 The greater problem perceived by participants seemed to be the attitude of the heritage Muslim male who considered that having sexual experience before marriage made a person dirty, or demonstrated a lack of good character. One participant reported that her marriage broke down over a phone call from an ex-boyfriend: 'My past (was) slapped back at me by my husband's remarks that, 'you can't help yourself chatting to men, can you?" Another participant recalled her husband's parents' difficulty in accepting their marriage because she was a previously married, single parent with two children. Citing the example of the Prophet, only one of whose wives was a virgin (the rest had been previously married), participants wondered why his example was not followed. Historically, it was considered a noble act for a man to marry a widowed woman and care for her and her children. This, it was felt, was another example of how subsequent cultural norms have infused Islamic precepts and have allowed distorted culturally-determined practices to take hold.

11.8 The socially constructed nature of ideas surrounding gender and sexuality has forced converts to confront cultural interpretations of sexuality. In some parts of the world it is common to view British men and women as drunken and promiscuous. Converts may become tainted by the actual or perceived behaviour of these men and women or by their own previous but now relinquished behaviour. Many assumptions which may be projected on to converts are founded on ignorance and prejudice, particularly those that perpetuate 'male myths of nymphomania'. One convert's prospective husband was told that 'you shouldn't marry a White woman; she will exhaust you in the bedroom'.

11.9 The extent to which converts were perceived to have 'looser' sexual morals than heritage Muslim women was discussed. One participant argued that, frequently, converts are perceived as easier to marry both because they are considered more sexually available and because of the lack of family protection from unsuitable partners. This may lead to marriages taking place without a serious intention of commitment on the part of the man. This can take the form of serial monogamy in which men readily marry and divorce, providing a means of engaging in sexually permissive behaviour, seemingly sanctioned through the contraction of a *nikah* (marriage contract). Failure to accord appropriate respect to a convert may also be demonstrated in other ways. A participant related that she was aware of Arabs who had married converts and had children but that these children were not always regarded as favourably as children born within subsequent marriages to Arab women.

11.10 A variety of sexual practices and preferences are openly represented within Western society, sometimes in ways which the participants felt to be overt and crude. However, while discussion and presentation of sex and sexuality outside certain bounds is less prevalent in Muslim communities, participants did not feel that this necessarily reflected the actual habits and practices of Muslims. The group discussed the high use of internet pornography particularly in Muslim countries with more reactionary social laws or traditions, which would appear to indicate a dichotomy in attitudes to sex, particularly in relation to Muslim men's view of women.[42]

11.11 Participants felt that the indulgence in any sexual behaviour that contravenes Islamic precepts receives undue emphasis and is more harshly judged by heritage Muslims than many other non-sexual forms of reprehensible behaviour.[43] Whether someone has committed other sins such as lying or back-biting, is rarely enquired into, along with the extent to which a person adheres to a generally moral code of behaviour.

11.12 Conversely, other participants spoke of men they knew, in some cases their own husbands, who did not display these attitudes towards the sexual experiences of a convert prior to her conversion to Islam. One participant mentioned that on marriage her heritage Muslim husband had said about her past, 'if you don't feel you need to tell me then I don't need to know'. It was felt that an Islamic marriage is based on a private and intimate relationship, the details of which are kept discreetly between the couple concerned. It was also asserted that the only time to be judgemental or generally discuss a person's character was when assessing them as a potential marriage partner.

11.13 Through conversion to Islam many converts have found it empowering not to have to conform to certain sexual stereotypes, including resisting the oppression of the fashion industry that can objectify and sexualise women. It was felt that representations of sexuality commonly promoted within British culture served to trivialise and ridicule sex and fails to locate sexual activity within safe parameters. Participants agreed that there is a general lack of societal recognition in the UK of the damaging and profound effects that unfettered sexuality can have on an individual's well-being and psychology.

11.14 The prevailing hyper-sexualisation of contemporary culture has led to some participants viewing this distortion of sexuality in Western society as a validation of their choice of Islam as a faith. To them, Islam offers dignity and modesty to women and the safe expression of sexuality within the security of marriage. One participant commented that she is constantly reassured of her conversion to Islam by looking at sexuality in contemporary Western society and at the normalisation of pornographic ideals of sexuality within it.

Pre-marital sexuality

11.15 Young educated female converts may wish to delay marriage in order to pursue career or other goals. In doing so, they may find it a challenge that all forms of sexual activity are denied them outside marriage by Islam. Those converts who desired an intimate sexual relationship but were deliberately delaying marriage for some other reasons, were led to question whether they have the strength to hold on to Islamic ideals.

11.16 Discussion ensued regarding what were the permitted outlets for sexual desire. It was agreed there was a need for services to counsel young or single people on how to manage sexual desire outside marriage alongside services to support marriage. It was found that converts need more guidance on what practices fall with the permitted bounds of Islam. They require knowledge as to how to deal with relationships with Muslim men before marriage, what, if any, forms of physical contact were permitted and whether dating was advisable. Participants discussed the new opportunities for meeting and developing relationships with potential partners which were not available for previous generations. It was felt that better mutual understanding between potential partners can help develop dialogue and communication as well as provide the basis for a lasting physical and emotional relationship among future partners.

11.17 One participant recognised the restrictions/restraints that Islam places upon an adherent's behaviour, stating that 'Islam is not for the faint-hearted' and that if one experiences weakness, Islam will strengthen them. Participants also called for a review of attitudes towards expectations and restrictions within marriage. The group offered the opinion that marriage is best viewed as an enabling relationship which allows each individual to give support to their partner and to lift and share the burdens of life, and that any attitude towards marriage as a constraint and limit to freedom was unhelpful.

12. Domestic violence

12.1 Violence perpetrated against Muslim women was described by one participant as 'one of our most uncomfortable secrets' and it was felt that issues concerning the abuse of women are 'swept under the carpet'. A helpline dealing with domestic abuse reported receiving calls from women experiencing violence in the home. The group identified a need for the development of organisations to support Muslim women when their marriages become unsustainable, particularly where violence and abuse is at issue, and to assist with exit strategies. This may involve the provision of refuges or safe houses, where women whose lives are at risk can seek sanctuary.

12.2 The reasons why those experiencing abuse within their relationships do not or cannot escape from the situation are complex, and not limited to women within Muslim communities. However, converts in particular may remain in abusive situations because of different or additional reasons, such as the lack of family support or because they may be reluctant to admit to their families that, after adopting another belief system and cultural code, the Muslim man they have married is an abusive husband. Such women are unlikely to find support within the Muslim community, where they are frequently instructed by community leaders to have patience, ignoring the injustice of the situation, its contradiction of Islamic principles and its criminality in Britain. The violence perpetrated towards convert women is often viewed by others as a sign of their own personal failings. These women are rebuked for 'not having sufficient knowledge to be a good, obedient wife.'

12.3 The experience of an abusive marriage was described by one participant, who will be called 'A' for the purposes of this report. 'A' converted to Islam aged sixteen and left home shortly afterward as her conversion distressed her mother. No assistance was provided by the heritage Muslim community. 'A' at first slept on the streets and then at the homes of friends. At this time she came to know a family whose son was looking to get married; the marriage was arranged without an opportunity for 'A' to fully understand her prospective husband or his family. Once married, 'A' was denied contact with her own family and confined to the house for four and a half years. On becoming pregnant the health of both 'A' and her child was at risk due to severe malnutrition. Confiding in her doctor, social services were informed of her condition and 'A' was taken into hospital for the remainder of her pregnancy. On giving birth she returned to her own family home. 'A's husband harassed her mother while she was living with her. As a result 'A' was forced to return to her marital home. Once there, violence from 'A''s husband intensified. On seeking help from within the community she was accused by those she sought help from of causing dishonour to her husband's family. 'A' eventually escaped from her husband's house with her two children, although the children were subsequently kidnapped by him during an access visit and taken to the Indian Subcontinent. 'A' has not seen her children for nine years. 'A' later remarried and has two further children with her second husband. 'A''s second husband has experienced difficulty in accepting that she was previously married and has not told his family of this previous marriage, nor of her two eldest children.

12.4 The situation above is an extreme and rare example of abuse within marriage, but it highlights the particular vulnerability of many converts to Islam. This vulnerability is demonstrated at several points. First, 'A' did not receive her family's support following her mother's reaction to her conversion. Second, as a convert without a support network within the Muslim community, 'A' was unable to access assistance within the community she had joined, and this made her vulnerable to the abuse of her husband and his family. Third, a lack of assistance from the community while the abuse was being perpetrated severely limited 'A''s ability to protect herself or her children either during or after her first marriage.

13. Polygyny

13.1 'Polygyny' describes the form of relationship in which a man enters into marriage with more than one wife. This term is more accurate in this context than the commonly used 'polygamy' which is not gender-specific: Islam does not permit a woman to marry more than one man at a time, whereas the Qur'an states that under certain conditions a man can marry up to four women. The Qur'an emphasises that it is better to have one wife, possibly recognising that plural marriages are likely to increase conflict and place more demands on all partners. If there is more than one wife, the Qur'an dictates that wives are to be treated by the husband with equality regardless of whether he feels more affection for one or some than for others.[44] The context of plural marriages within the Qur'an makes it clear that this is intended as a means to provide for the welfare of divorced, abandoned or widowed women and their children, who are considered orphans.

13.2 The Prophet Muhammad engaged in both a monogamous marriage and, following the death of his first wife, in plural marriages. These plural marriages were contracted for a variety of reasons, including to secure political alliances between conflicting tribes and to set an example of the virtue of marrying women who were widowed, thereby providing them with financial support, protection and social standing within society. This was considered a noble act. Plural marriages were also used as a solution within periods of history in which women outnumbered men, in order to provide economic and social security. It was permitted to divorce a wife if she could not provide children, but also considered kinder to remain married to her while contracting a second marriage. Some of these conditions may not be present in Britain; this fact calls for a new assessment of absolutist interpretations of polygyny.

13.3 Some participants considered that a few converts promote a submissive, subjugated role for women by actively seeking to be second, rather than first, wives. It was agreed that some women may possess character traits which do not lead them to seek intense and possessive personal relationships. A case illustrating this is of a convert Muslim woman who did not object to her wealthy non-British husband marrying a single parent because she was concerned for the woman's welfare and that of her children, as they were living in a country without a welfare state.

13.4 Some of the participants did not view the decision to enter into a plural marriage as a retrograde step, but as an equally valid and informed choice which might allow educated women to enter into a form of marriage that enabled them to enjoy the intimacy and protection of a man, without the full-time responsibility of meeting the needs of a marital partner. A half, or a third or a quarter of a husband (if he had the full cohort of four wives) seemed preferable to some participants, because it afforded them the time and freedom to pursue their own lives and interests. Others viewed such attitudes as being demeaning, or as being merely a smokescreen to conceal a lack of self-esteem and self-worth.

13.5 Some participants found the idea of plural marriage distasteful and harmful to women. Concern was expressed for women already involved in the marriage and the possible distress caused to them by their husbands taking additional wives. It was mentioned that the Prophet Muhammad discouraged his son-in-law Ali from taking a second wife after seeing his daughter Fatima visibly distressed at the prospect, on the grounds that 'I hate what she hates to see, and what hurts her, hurts me'.[45]

13.6 One participant questioned whether it was necessary or desirable for the convert to relinquish Western cultural notions of marriage, romance and love. Most participants felt that plural marriages were undesirable and considered themselves attached to the Western cultural ideal of marriage as a monogamous relationship between a single woman and a single man, based on initial affection or love.

13.7 Whether aspects of polygyny might provide the opportunity for spiritual growth and development was explored. Some argued that polygyny may encourage women to master the jealous tendencies and negative emotions that might arise from sharing a husband. The negative reactions of women within plural marriages might be avoided through the husband's sensitivity and by treating his wives with equity and fairness. However, some participants considered that entering into plural marriages displayed selfish tendencies on the part of both the husband and the new wife and that it indicated a lack of empathy for the woman already within the marriage.

13.8 Participants also discussed the transferability of such a practice to a different time and culture, where such a practice is often viewed with distaste or ridicule. Converts engaged in plural marriages may need to explain polygyny to their own families who may well be unfamiliar with such practices and their position within Islam. While some families are accepting of polygynous choices, these may often create unease and disquiet for family members. This in turn may lead to converts not publicly acknowledging their involvement in a plural marriage to avoid provoking adverse responses, both from their families and from the wider public.

13.9 One participant cited the example of a plural marriage she was aware of where the women worked together and were companions for each other. A further example was discussed of a Saudi woman unable to have children. She had established a good relationship with her husband's second wife, with whom she helped to raise her husband's children. It was considered that, given the context of Saudi society, it would have been far more damaging for her if her husband had divorced her than it was for her to accept him marrying another woman.

13.10 Any plural marriages made in Britain do not exist within any British legal framework and so no formal security or stability is available for the women and children involved. Women contracting marriages as subsequent wives do not receive any civil recognition of their relationship or status. This may lead to secrecy, with women being able to present themselves as being married only in certain circumstances and being forced to deny their marriages in certain other contexts.

13.11 A participant stressed the importance of marriage contracts that outline the conditions of marriage and the entitlements that the husband and wife wish to include. The participant described her marriage, which took place in Pakistan. On her father-in-law's insistence a marriage contract was drawn up into which he inserted a clause preventing her husband from taking a second wife.

13.12 A personal experience of polygyny was shared by one participant (here called 'B'). 'B' had married a heritage, non-practising Muslim and had three children with him. Subsequent to the marriage he became a practising Muslim and developed concerns over his wife's sexual experiences previous to marriage. He was advised by an Imam to take a second wife. On 'B' refusing to sanction this arrangement the marriage deteriorated further and ended in divorce. This has left her feeling disillusioned with Muslim men; her second marriage was to a non-Muslim who later decided to convert to Islam.

13.13 Other participants rejected the concept of plural marriage as the following statements reveal: 'I can't imagine being with a man who I had to share. Can't imagine being with a man who was sleeping with another woman'. 'I think polygamy is disgusting – it is dirty'. Some participants argued that there was nothing wrong with being an unmarried Muslim woman; a fulfilling life could still be led. 'You don't have to settle for that quality of life'. A participant stated that there are many historical examples of prominent, respected Muslim men and women who have remained unmarried. 'It is not an absolute obligation to be married, nor should you be expected to become a mother following marriage', one participant said.

13.14 Polygyny was also discussed as a response to the desperation and loneliness that older women in particular may experience when opportunities for marriage appear to be dwindling. Polygyny may offer them the chance to enter into a married relationship. Participants considered this to be a less than ideal form of relationship but one that might be preferable to loneliness.

13.15 Polygyny is frequently suggested to older converts as a possible solution to the lack of eligible unmarried men. A participant who maintained that she did not wish to become involved with polygyny mentioned the difficulty of finding a husband. This can become a particularly onerous test of faith for older unmarried converts, especially if they wish to have children. This for one participant created an uncomfortable awareness that had it not been for her conversion she might have chosen to have a child outside marriage. Some converts, failing to find a suitable Muslim partner, may seek to marry outside their new faith. This choice, although not a widely accepted practice, may be increasing. Improved social education could assist in revising the attitudes of men and their families towards some convert women who are largely considered to be unsuitable marriage partners due to their age or marital or sexual history.

14. Divorced women

14.1 A participant described how difficult she had found integrating with heritage Muslims after her divorce, having been much more easily accepted when she first embraced Islam. Another participant commented that because a divorced woman was perceived to have failed at marriage she was expected to fail at her faith and to abandon it.[46] Participants raised the difficulty of obtaining a *khul'* (wife-initiated) form of divorce. 'No one wants to help you', one said.

14.2 Divorced convert women, despite the Prophetic example of marrying older, previously married women, largely fail to receive assistance in finding second husbands from heritage Muslims, apart from those men with dubious motives designed to secure access to money or passports. One participant who entered Islam at the same time as she divorced her non-Muslim husband wishes for marriage, but feels that no avenues are open to her to find a suitable partner; she is merely advised to fast and get on with her life.

14.3 One divorced participant found, following the breakdown of her marriage to a Muslim man, that a large part of her Islamic lifestyle had derived from the marriage. The divorce resulted in the loss of a large part of her support network. She described herself as being 'a spiritual hermit', alone and isolated from an established Muslim community. A test of the strength of faith can often come following the breakdown of a relationship or marriage. A number of the participants had retained their faith following the collapse of their marriages and were able to separate their faith from their marriage.[47]

14.4 Another participant stated that she had remained within an unhappy marriage because she did not want to jeopardize her daughters' marriage prospects within Muslim communities by joining the ranks of the socially excluded, in this case, divorced women. Such a consideration was thought unwise by other participants, who questioned why a convert would want to marry her daughters to men who thought and acted in this way. Nonetheless, this participant considered the merits of remaining married to be exemplified on Eid, when her seven year old grandson led the prayers, and where she sees all her children and grandchildren, who are Arabic-speaking, practising Muslims.

15. Converts' children

15.1 Most of the participants who were married had brought up or were bringing up children in cross-cultural marriages. Frequently, children of these parents had learned to see the world from a variety of cultural perspectives, giving them grounding in empathy with those from different cultural frames of reference. Participants found that issues surrounding their children's identity were often confusing, but were resolved over time. Conflicting issues over identity may be partly due to the (normal) adolescent identity-crises of teenage development rather than to unresolved uncertainties over Islam. One participant mentioned how her children had to struggle for their sense of belonging wherever they were residing; when they were living abroad they were regarded as 'the English Muslim kids', and when in England as 'the Arab Muslim kids'. In terms of their understanding of their faith and beliefs, a participant quoted her son's comment that he will decide for himself how he wants to express his Islamic faith: 'I am not defined by who my parents are', he stated.

15.2 The African-Caribbean participants stated that their children frequently found it difficult to maintain the full practice of Islam. A new young British Black Muslim identity has started to emerge in Britain today, mixed with other youth identities. However, participants noted that it is becoming more common for marriages to take place between children of African-Caribbean heritage and those of South Asian heritage. Younger age groups are breaking down barriers, and racial prejudices between different ethnic groups are often less pronounced or pervasive than those held by older generations. Participants felt that there is still a long way to go and that frequently the children of African-Caribbean convert Muslims find Islam unattractive due to the differences they perceive between their mother's position as a woman in Islam and the prevalence of racism and prejudice displayed by heritage Muslims towards non-White converts and their families. However, as the participants' children matured, many returned to practising Islam.

15.3 The religious education of children was also shown to present problems for converts. One participant described how she had established a supplementary school to teach children about Islam, learning herself alongside the children. Prior to this, she had sent her eldest two children to a mosque but they suffered in two ways: they could not understand the teaching owing to the fact that it was in Urdu, and they were physically disciplined.

This raised her awareness of the need to find suitable Islamic teaching for her children. The participant described how her daughter was now studying Arabic at university and teaching the language to her mother.

15.4 One participant of African-Caribbean heritage recounted her daughter's 'worst experience in life' when attending a Muslim school as a child. The Asian children brought their racism and prejudice to school, and she suffered badly as a result. The participant stated that she was unaware at the time of the racial bullying her daughter was enduring at school, which has led her daughter to have a negative view of Muslims.

15.5 One participant had successfully raised her sons to be bilingual in English and Arabic and they had received a good Islamic education, partly delivered by their father. The family resided for a while in North Africa, where the children were teased at school because they had a Christian mother, and where their father was publicly asked to divorce his wife because she was Christian. During their local (state) education in England, the children again received racist taunts at school, but it was not until her sons were well into adulthood that they revealed to their parents the extent to which they had suffered. Muslims were regarded as a nuisance by some schools, which made no concessions for their religious needs. For example, following sports activities at school they were allowed to enter the shower last (as it is not permissible for Muslims to take communal showers) but given detention when they were late to classes as a result.

15.6 One participant described the paths that her three children have followed now that they have reached adulthood. Her eldest son took a Western interpretation of Islam, in terms of his friendships and behaviour. He did not feel that it was important to identify with the Arab side of his heritage and identified himself as English. The second son identified strongly with his Arab Muslim heritage and participated in the armed revolution against the dictatorship previously controlling his father's country. The third child considered herself a Muslim, in a more measured way. She has developed a strong sense of her own identity, independent of her parents' heritage.

15.7 One participant described growing up as the child of a convert to Islam who had married a man from Bangladesh. 'When I was good I was the Bengali child, when I did something wrong I was the child of that convert woman. I was uncertain as to my identity, regarding who I was and who I wasn't', she said. Her mother was an outspoken English woman who converted to Islam, and subsequently went to live in Bangladesh, where she was treated as a trophy, but told that she was not a proper Muslim. 'These events put me off Islam,' the participant said, and it was only years later that she returned to practice Islam, encouraged by her enjoyment of the company of other converts.

15.8 It was suggested that where a marriage has taken place between a Muslim father and a Christian mother the children are often more happy within the Christian cultural side of the family, perhaps because the children are not made to feel so coerced into becoming 'practicing Christians' and they can more light-heartedly enjoy occasions centred around children, such as Christmas, with presents.

15.9 In terms of the friendships subsequently formed by converts' children, one participant mentioned that 'now my children are older they have a few distant Muslim friends'. Their close friends are all non-Muslims, because they could not tolerate the behaviour of the many Muslims who go adrift, with little supervision or support from their families, and may end up imprisoned.

15.10 Many identity issues were found to be common to dual heritage children. These children are both different from their mothers and different from their fathers and as such will have experiences dissimilar to those of their parents. One participant mentioned her concern that, due to their Western upbringing, her children would not be able to adapt to the cultural expectations of marriage within an Arab context when they became older. 'Who am I bringing them up to be fit to be married to?' she asked.

15.11 The participants raising children on their own as single parents described the difficulties of trying to impart a faith identity and knowledge to their children, while being the principle breadwinners in their family and, therefore, simultaneously trying to manage the responsibilities of parenting, coupled with running a home. One participant who had three children when she converted to Islam, described how the eldest had become antagonistic towards Islam, which had deepened his sense of a British-Christian identity, although not in a particularly religious sense. Her younger children, born after her conversion to Islam, received little Islamic education due to the lack of support. Another participant who had a large family reiterated these sentiments, outlining the challenge she had faced raising her children and instilling them with a love of Islam. One of her children, now an adult, would not class himself as a Muslim and the rest were practising Islam to varying degrees. During her children's upbringing this participant had been unable to afford the school fees to send them to an Islamic school and was unable to teach them Arabic. The lack of a father to supervise her sons meant that when attending Islamic events, which are largely segregated, she had often had to leave her sons at home, which meant that they had missed out on opportunities to socialise with other Muslims. Events staged by a Muslim project had proven to be helpful in introducing her daughters to other Muslims, enabling friendships to develop. The support and help she had encountered in coping as a single parent had come from non-Muslims and she had found the heritage Muslim communities unsupportive of her needs.

15.12 Participants noted that the lack of sufficient Islamic input into children's education was not a problem facing single parents alone. One participant who had been married to a male convert stated that her son grew up with little Islamic education; supplementary school did not prove successful and, now in his mid-twenties, he is not a practising Muslim and the friends he associates with are not Muslim.

15.13 The lack of familial support for converts with children was a constant theme throughout the symposia. This was exacerbated for the disabled, where support was scant. Difficulties in dealing with a disabled child often placed intolerable strain on marriages and, too frequently, mothers were left raising disabled children on their own. Mosques rarely provided facilities for disabled people, who were often stigmatized within heritage Muslim communities; this served to further isolate mothers struggling to cope with disabled children.

15.14 Some parents were seen to take a harsh, uncompromising approach to raising children in Britain, failing to take account of the cultural influences that impact their child's perceptions of activities that they wish to engage in. These parents seem to stamp out all life from their children by forbidding television and music. It was seen as important to raise children who were able to deal effectively with the society that surrounds them, while having at the same time an awareness of the importance of faith in their lives. A participant mentioned the need to find alternative activities for children, if parents wanted to deter them from being interested in something they considered unsuitable. The importance of providing a good example to children was mentioned, along with listening to them, letting children express their own opinions and spending time with them.

15.15 It was considered essential to remember that the children of converts are likely to have a less intense relationship with Islam than their parents and that those children need to arrive at their own understanding of how to practice their faith as they become adults. The following poem was offered to the participants as advice and wisdom on bringing up children.

> **ON CHILDREN BY KHALIL GIBRAN**
>
> Your children are not your children.
> They are the sons and daughters of life's longing for itself.
> They come through you but not from you,
> And though they are with you yet they belong not to you.
>
> You may give them your love but not your thoughts,
> For they have their own thoughts.
> You may house their bodies but not their souls,
> For their souls dwell in the house of tomorrow,
> Which you cannot visit, not even in your dreams.
> You may strive to be like them,
> But seek not to make them like you.
> For life goes not backward nor tarries with yesterday.
>
> You are the bows from which your children
> As living arrows are sent forth.
> The archer sees the mark upon the path of the infinite
> And he bends you with his might
> That his arrows may go far and swift.
> Let your bending in the archer's hand be for gladness;
> For even as he loves the arrow that flies,
> So he loves the bow that is stable

16. Homosexuality

16.1 A number of the participants felt themselves to be tuned in with variations in sexuality. These participants were openly accepting of homosexuals and wanted to see inclusive interpretations of Islam appropriate for all people, and which would not exclude the participation of gay and lesbian Muslims. The majority of the participants argued that every person is formed by the design of God and, therefore, deserves to be treated with respect and dignity, but that sexual acts, such as sodomy, are forbidden in Islam. One participant commented: 'If I come across a homosexual who wants to be a Muslim, I say 'it is between you and Allah." Maybe it is just as difficult to stop backbiting, overeating or any of the other vices that take us away from Allah.

16.2 Participants felt that stereotypical presentations of Muslims by the media propagate the message that the normal response of Muslims is to hate homosexuals. Muslims may become the proxy for sentiments that are not exclusive to sectors of the Muslim communities, but are prevalent throughout society but difficult to express. Some participants found gay lobby groups aggressive and considered their dominant role in the media to have contributed to a political climate that curtails people from expressing disapproval of homosexual acts without being labelled discriminatory.

16.3 When discussing homosexuality, participants questioned whether they had the right to speak on behalf of someone whose sexuality they could, in terms of its social consequences, empathise with but did not share. Converts may be ideally placed to share the experience of being outsiders and learn valuable lessons on issues surrounding exclusion and inclusion, acceptance and rejection. Empathy does not, however, necessarily equate with acceptance. The majority of participants felt that, while discussion may focus on mercy and acceptance, in Islam there is only one sanctioned form of intimate relationship, that is, between a husband and a wife.

16.4 Many participants had experience of more liberal views before conversion than the views they now confront towards homosexuality within the heritage Muslim community. One participant stated that her liberal atheist family of origin would have preferred her to be gay than to have converted to Islam. Being gay was seen by them to be acceptable, whereas adopting a religious faith was not.

16.5 Although the provision for capital punishment exists within Islamic law for acts of homosexuality, the necessity of providing four witnesses to sexual acts has largely precluded such punishments from being dealt out. Participants discussed the view that, historically, Muslim societies adopted a different approach to homosexuality than the West. Prohibitions in the Qur'an against suspicion and spying have led more generally to toleration regarding private personal matters.[48] In the past, homosexuals were commonly able to live undisturbed in Islamic societies, in comparison to Europe where more prying cultural intrusion leading to punishment, including the death penalty, was not uncommon.

16.6 A number of participants involved in counselling and help-lines described the situation of gay Muslims struggling with their faith and sexuality. In particular they discussed lesbian converts. Homosexual Muslims were frequently shunned and rejected by heritage Muslim communities. In some cases, ignorant and perilous advice had been given to homosexuals by other Muslims, such as that they should throw themselves off the nearest parapet.

16.7 Traditionally within Muslim societies homosexuality has not been treated with the level of disdain with which it now meets. Gay Muslims now felt compelled to choose between their sexuality and their faith, which are viewed as irreconcilable. A participant described a friend who had discovered that her son was gay and had sought advice regarding how she should deal with his sexuality in order to allow him to remain within the Muslim community. It was considered possible by participants to disagree with the sexual behaviour of homosexual men and lesbian women, but to acknowledge and respect them as human beings, while treating them with compassion and mercy.

16.8 Many gay and lesbian Muslims feel that their sexuality is genetically rather than socially determined. Some participants commented that young people who are spiritually tortured by their sexuality often come from 'good Muslim backgrounds'. There is a marked refusal within the Muslim community to offer appropriate advice and to address the concerns of homosexuals. However, participants felt that homosexual activity was not always the result of purely genetic factors, citing anecdotal cases of female prisoners who, trapped in an environment largely devoid of men, frequently develop lesbian relationships with other prisoners. Many of these women respond to the environment in which they have been placed by adopting sexual behaviour they would not otherwise have engaged in; many are in heterosexual relationships when not incarcerated. For many female prisoners, including Muslims, this behaviour is triggered by the prison environment. It was also mentioned that such a response to single-sex incarceration has been recognised as contributing to the development of homosexuality in male prisoners and all-male crews of sea-going vessels.

17. Trans-sexualism

17.1 Issues surrounding trans-sexualism were introduced into the discussion, largely on the basis of the experiences of one participant.[49] As personal experience and representation were limited to a sole voice, it was not easy to assess how representative the experiences described were of transsexual converts to Islam in Britain, or more generally of heritage Muslims. Informative insights were provided, and the narrative gave the participants the opportunity to consider perspectives on sexuality and exclusion that they might not previously have encountered. Cultural practices relating to trans-sexualism within several Muslim countries were also discussed.

17.2 The participant concerned was born as a man, but during early childhood identified clearly with femininity, rather than masculinity. 'I tried to be a normal lad', she said. As a man he had converted to Islam, married a Muslim woman and had fathered two children. Years of wrestling with the complicated issues arising from sexuality, which she maintains were not the result of a lifestyle choice but part of her biology, ensued. Her sexual identity was medically attributed to the hormone flow to her as a foetus. The decision to undergo a gender changing operation had proved a difficult one for the family to negotiate. At the transitional stage of changing from a man into a woman, the participant had sought the support of heritage Muslim communities, but found that she was shunned. 'It just freaks them out', she said. The lack of support, compounded by a number of major personal issues to address, such as the death of her mother and the stress of caring for her father, led to a mental breakdown.

17.3 Prior to the gender alignment surgery, the participant had lived as a male convert in a Muslim country. As a skilled male professional, she was treated with great respect and it was wonderful for her to be a Muslim and to fit into society. This treatment contrasted starkly with the apparent disdain and revulsion that the participant experienced in Britain from heritage Muslim communities following surgery to become a woman. The rejection described led not to bitterness but to an awareness that it had enabled her to see things in a different way, and which gave her alternative perspectives on faith, people and life. She now describes herself as reconciled and complete as a person. She feels particularly close to God when she takes solitary walks in the country, being at one with nature and with the source of life.

17.4 The strict gender segregation that is kept in mosques in the UK proved a further barrier to this transgender convert's participation in Muslim community life. The participant wished for a change allowing Muslims to pray together regardless of their gender. She felt that true focus on the divine would act as a barrier to any sexual distraction from obstructing the prayers; when present in a mosque there was a need to rise above sexuality and seek contact with God. However, another participant welcomed segregation, as she found the presence of men distracting and that it prevented her from concentrating on her faith.

17.5 The transgendered participant currently lives with her former wife in a platonic relationship maintained through friendship in Muslim life. The former wife is concerned not to be considered a lesbian, coming from a country where the death penalty is administered to homosexuals. Isolation from the mainstream heritage Muslim community has led to a reassessment of the participant's relationship with Islam. She believes strongly in God and the Qur'an as the word of God and in the existence of the Prophet Muhammad, but deeply questions the authenticity of some *hadith*. The participant considers that her relationship with God now transcends traditional understandings of Islam, although she believes she remains a Muslim. She maintains that her faith has developed to a higher level of consciousness, focused on a universalistic understanding of spirituality.

17.6 For Muslims deviating from the accepted norms adhered to by mainstream communities, the social and psychological costs are high. The participating transgender convert had been ostracised from the heritage Muslim community to such an extent that she now refuses to enter a mosque and shies away from engaging at any level with Muslims. Her participation at the symposium required repeated assurances that she would be treated with dignity and respect.

17.7 The participant saw her situation as representing the need for recognition of a third gender.[50] Along the spectrum from male to female there are many people who are in the middle, like hermaphrodites. She described the *ruh*, the spirit present in all humans as bisexual, and representative of the Taoist concepts of '*yinyang*'.[51] Others see the *ruh*, as asexual rather than bisexual. For this participant, the spirit being of neither gender but present in all people was illustrative of the need to develop beyond the binary categorisations of male and female.

17.8 One participant described meeting a gregarious transsexual woman in the women's section at a Sufi event. The heritage Muslim women present appeared to be accepting of the woman, but raised concerns over whether they could pray alongside her, or could remove their headscarves in front of her. The participant did not have enough Islamic knowledge to address their questions.

18. Gender

18.1 The symposia discussed the idea of equitable relations between Muslim men and women, and considered how appropriate it is to discuss gender in the context of contemporary British society. The discussion compared issues of concern for Muslim women with the position of non-Muslim women in Britain today. This was a useful comparison to make because all the participants were resident in Britain. Western perspectives on gender were not perceived by participants to be the benchmarks by which gender relations within Muslim communities should be measured. One participant said that she had 'a great deal of criticism, as a British woman, of Western standards, which are very inequitable to women.' Such criticism of British society had not been created by her relationship with Islam, but was part of her view on women in society that she had brought with her into Islam. This participant objected to Western perspectives on gender roles and relationships and did not consider them worthy of emulation. She argued that the only thing Islam has to be judged against is the comparative human standard of decency. Here, participants' questions focused on how a society should operate to ensure the equity and dignity of all its members. A participant mentioned that a factor that had strongly influenced her when entering Islam was the idea that a woman's life is not pre-ordained and prescribed as a social category.

18.2 A number of participants questioned Western assumptions of equality which they felt leave many women unfairly burdened with the responsibilities of running a home, working, and child care, along with pressure to assume a sexualised presentation of the Self. It was considered that Western concepts of gender were flawed. Western women had been deceived by feminist discourses based largely on the angst and concerns of White middle class European women. Pursuing notions of equality had perpetuated inequalities. The notion of equity was lost in the pursuit of equality. Some participants thought that Western understandings of equity are problematic and deserve to be questioned, considering instead that Islam had established equity as an ideal which allows for compatibility between the roles of men and women. Suffragettes in Britain had to fight long and hard to achieve some of the rights that were enshrined within Islamic law. Many verses in the Qur'an explicitly address both men and women simultaneously, outlining their responsibilities within society and a number describe the mutual responsibility for both men and women to play an active and meaningful role in society. It was felt that contemporary Islamic scholarship lacks an awareness and acknowledgement of the roles actually fulfilled by women. In many early Islamic societies, educated women taught men, just as educated men taught women and there was not a segregated system of learning. It was noted by participants that contemporary Moroccan scholars have sought to reassess and reinterpret the *Sharia*, in order to ensure equality for women.

18.3 The dignity and respect that the Qur'an affords to both men and women is currently being explored through exegesis undertaken by female commentators. This emphasis on female scholarship does not preclude the equal consideration of the insights of inquiring men regarding the contextualisation of Islam and its relevance to contemporary life. However, the extent to which contemporary female exegesis of the Qur'an is influencing women is uncertain. It has been difficult for converts to have access to less traditional interpretations of the Qur'an, simply because such interpretations have been marginal to the life of most Muslims across Europe and the world. The domination of traditional scholarship has shut out much of the diversity of thought inherent in the understanding and practice of Islam. This is not to negate the value of traditional thought but the relevance of traditional world views needs to be enhanced by their incorporation into contemporary life. Participants felt a need for scholarship that can both encompass and transcend the worldview of 7th century Arabia and the early history of Islam in the Middle East, thus making Islam not merely accessible but also able to relate to the varied needs of many different Muslims throughout the world. Most of the early Muslims were converts, and as such played a vital role in the development of the faith and its dissemination across the world.

18.4 One participant told the group that a heritage Muslim in a bookshop had tried to deter her from purchasing a Qur'anic exegesis written by an American female scholar. How a convert is able to think about Islam is partially determined by the access they have to a wide range of differing perspectives. It often takes determination to access a text that assists in the development of more far-sighted approaches to learning and teaching. One participant mentioned attending a *fiqh* class in London, where the first topic for discussion was how to deal with a rat found in a cooking bowl. The answer was to bury the rat, wash the bowl seven times in sand and say a special prayer, rather than to ring Kensington and Chelsea pest control. This lack of ability to transfer precepts relevant to a 7th century desert society to a contemporary European one is indicative of the inability on the part of some Islamic authorities to provide appropriate responses to the needs of both convert and heritage Muslims in the modern global world.

18.5 Participants recognised a failure within the more restricted debates offered by Muslim scholars to advance discussion on women's issues. This has largely focused on rather stale issues such as women's roles, rights and dress. Internet sites perpetuate the lists of 'rules' derived from Qur'anic verses pertaining to women. Such approaches, 'lack conceptual context' and make the 'lists of do's and don'ts meaningless, except as a bulwark for questionable tradition'. The group felt a need to move away from this prescriptive approach of women fitting into a pre-ordained order, towards a better understanding of how God considers them to fit into the universe.

18.6 Participants felt that the breadth of issues that are encompassed under the social term 'gender' are frequently seized upon by non-Muslims to illustrate supposed inherent weaknesses of the Islamic faith. Participants felt that Muslims are often used as a proxy to discuss a range of issues that in fact occur with more frequency within other cultures, than amongst Muslims. For instance, honour killings and forced marriages are found in Hindu communities. Female genital mutilation is a feature of many African societies, including Christian ones. The connection of these practices with Islam and Muslims only serves to keep a constant drip feed of negative media focus on Islam. To use the example of forced marriages, these have come to be equated specifically with Islam in the minds of the general public in Britain, rather than being recognised as a concern within a number of communities and cultures. There is a widespread acceptance in Britain of the idea that Islam is oppressive to women. This serves to remove the spotlight from other faiths with anti-female traditions. For instance, Jewish men pray daily, 'thank God I am not born a woman.'

18.7 One participant considered that where women do receive unjust treatment due to cultural practices, women are complicit in the denial of their

God-given rights due to a failure to collectively hold men to account. This, it was pointed out, may unfairly assume that women have more power to effect change than it is reasonable to expect. Nonetheless, it was felt that some women collude in their own oppression.

18.8 One participant was of the opinion that it is women who raise and indulge male children and enable them to be treated in a different way from female children. While accounting for the responsibility that women have to equitably socialise their children, it was felt that this explanation did not adequately recognise the power structures that marginalise women and operate to their detriment. Women may be particularly subject to oppression through poverty, race or class prejudice and poor access to resources. Nevertheless, some felt that it is a false analogy to look at women as a separate group, distinct from the problems which, in many situations, they share with men. To stereotype women as a separate class or group, defined by their femininity, may deny them their individuality and personalities. There is, therefore, a necessity to provide a more robust framework allowing for access to equity and social justice for all men and women in society.

18.9 Islam is a moral and questioning path which provides for immense diversity of thought and practice within Islamic societies. This dynamic and context-sensitive understanding of Islam is largely obscured by public debate, and needs to be brought to the forefront of these debates. This means allowing for the possibility of 'doing things differently to do things the same'. The Qur'an is written in a dynamic form and the *Sharia* is open to interpretation and reinterpretation. The struggle both for converts and heritage Muslims is finding appropriate ways to practice Islam within the society and culture in which they live.

18.10 Culture can become a veil that obscures Islam, allowing a view of a specific culture, but not of Islam. Many women find the ideals of Islam empowering but find that the reality of the culturally-infused practices labelled as 'Islamic', engaged in by sections of the heritage Muslim communities, appears to be more regressive and oppressive. There is a constant tension between purely Islamic ideals and the culturally-infused behaviour of the various ethnic Muslims.

18.11 A common misconception is that the practices of segregating men and women necessarily operate to the detriment of women. Separated and segregated societies do not necessarily decree submissive and secondary roles for women. Women have powerful spheres of influence and control in their own domains, as demonstrated by matriarchal societies.

19. Becoming part of wider Muslim communities

19.1 The participants discussed how their conversions had been received by heritage Muslim communities. There was consensus that taking the *shahada* is a warmly celebrated and welcomed event. While everyone rushes to congratulate the new convert, often they are subsequently largely left to their own devices, making them frequently struggle to find a comfortable niche within the heritage Muslim communities. Participants noted the tendency for converts to be regarded as 'trophy' Muslims and paraded in a tokenistic fashion. They are alternately regarded as people whose opinions are called upon, and also as people who need to be constantly instructed and reminded of the 'rules' of the religion, and how these should be applied. The interest on the part of heritage Muslims appeared to be in the process of changing a person into a Muslim, or indoctrinating them into following a particular interpretation of Islam, rather than in meeting the needs of the convert. It was felt that the positive aspects of the convert's cultural heritage are neither appreciated nor understood, but instead derided and expected to be discarded. The convert was encouraged to reject who they were and where they had come from.

19.2 It was felt that the taking of the *shahada* by converts serves to bolster and legitimise Islam in the eyes of heritage Muslims living in Western countries where it has become both publicly and institutionally acceptable to denigrate and deride Islam. In this context White British converts are welcomed into the faith; their conversion represents a triumph of Islam over the indigenous culture. One participant commented on the remarks that a heritage Muslim had addressed to her, that she was an exceptionally fine Muslim woman because she had chosen Islam rather than having inherited it from her parents. Her response was that 'you can't inherit faith; we all have to choose to submit to Islam'.

19.3 The White convert is often used for *dawa* discussions, exhibitions on Islam and new Muslim programmes. 'They become like the family's best china, only taken out when the vicar comes to tea', one participant said. 'You may admire the trophy but you do not necessarily want to display it on your mantelpiece.' The view of the convert as a trophy is more apparent in the cases of converts from high profile backgrounds, such as the musician Cat Stevens, who became known as Yusuf Islam after conversion. The prestige with which a convert like Yusuf Islam is regarded becomes an additional source of pride and validation for heritage Muslims. For the majority of White converts, however, being regarded as a trophy is no more than a symbolic gesture. Few converts go on to hold positions of authority within Muslim communities or organisations, and many struggle to gain any meaningful form of acceptance within heritage Muslim communities.

19.4 Converts of African-Caribbean heritage stated that they were not viewed as 'trophies' and that their conversions remained invisible, uncelebrated and frequently unacknowledged. They faced a huge struggle to be acknowledged as Muslims, and had to fight to gain acceptance within mosques and in heritage Muslim communities. This was considered to be due to the low status that Black people are generally accorded among heritage Muslim communities. Judgements on the value of Muslims according to their skin colour runs counter to the ideals of Islam where piety rather than race accords status.

19.5 The participants discussed the extent to which notions of the convert as a trophy are specific to Islam or have wider applicability to other belief systems. Participants cited examples of evangelical Christians using new recruits to their form of Christianity in a similar way. It was thought that this was unlikely to be the case within Judaism, as the acceptance of a convert into Judaism is complex in different ways. As a faith Judaism appears to be somewhat hesitant about conversion, making the process difficult or, in some interpretations of the faith, almost impossible to achieve.

Perceptions of how heritage Muslims view British culture

19.6 Comments were made to the effect that often within Muslim communities being 'of White British heritage' is perceived as even more valuable than being a heritage Muslim; this is indicative of the crisis of confidence experienced by Muslims in Britain. Being a Muslim is not seen as a position to aspire to. This reflects a denigration of the value, worth and culture of Muslims. Because White- and Western- are perceived to be best, when a White Westerner chooses Islam it appears to validate Islam as a religion. It becomes apparent that there are two contradictory strands of thought operating in tandem. On the one hand White and Western are seen to be superior. On the other hand the culture these elements represent is often disparaged by heritage Muslims as inferior.

19.7 By way of contrast, historical antecedents reveal a time when being Arab was an honour and Islamic culture was emulated. It is reported that the headmaster of Westminster public school (private/independent) would tell parents, 'send us your English boys and we will return them to you as Arabs'. Islam and Muslims continue to fascinate British people but at the same time are viewed with a level of disdain. Several participants mentioned how disturbed they feel about the portrayal of Western society by some heritage Muslims. 'I hate it when people go on about kafirs – that's my mum, my dad, my sister and they are better people than half the Muslims I have met,' commented one participant. She added: 'If I see a dawa stall in the street, I don't want to hear about the kuffar – I don't want to hear my family described like this. It's not about putting other people down. How can a majority population see Islam in a positive light if it is constantly subjected to hearing that their system is not good enough and needs to be replaced?' It was, however, acknowledged that 'there are huge discrepancies between what Islam is about and how it is lived.' To non-Muslims, the way Muslims behave appears representative of Islam. They are not equipped to identify the distinction between culture and Islam.

19.8 British society is regarded negatively by some Muslims, and this impacts the perceptions projected on converts to Islam, who find it difficult to counteract the stereotypes that may be applied personally to them, towards their families, or to the wider British society. More disturbing is the transmutation of such attitudes into a profound lack of regard for the well-being of non-Muslim women. There are many cases of Muslim men taking advantage of non-Muslim women for sexual encounters whilst at university, before they enter into arranged marriages with Muslim women. The attitude displayed by heritage Muslims who were involved in criminal activity towards non-Muslim women is too often related to prejudicial views that border on racism. Several of the participants referred to recent cases of young British girls, of varying ethnic backgrounds but predominantly White, who had been groomed into prostitution by men of Muslim origin, and who had subsequently suffered violence, abuse and exploitation as a result.

19.9 It was felt that the sexualisation and commoditisation of young non-Muslim women influences how converts are perceived by Muslim communities to be 'bringing bad blood into the community'. One participant asked why converts were not expressing their concern about the ill treatment of girls exploited within the Muslim community. It may be too simplistic to link pejorative views of non-Muslim women to criminal behaviour carried out by nominally Muslim men. In response, it was pointed out that abuse and exploitation cross ethnic and religious borders and are the result of a complex mix of social conditions including disenfranchisement, poverty, vulnerability, powerlessness and criminality.

Becoming part of Muslim communities

19.10 Following the decision to convert to Islam the challenge for many converts has been how to become part of a Muslim community without necessarily adopting the ethnic culture of the community to which the convert has become attached. Converts' attempts to join established Muslim communities are characterised by varying degrees of success, depending on the types of Muslim groups or organisations that they encounter. If a convert becomes a Muslim as part of a multicultural community of Muslims, which occurs more commonly in parts of London and other larger cities in the UK, the need to form an allegiance to a particular culture may not occur.

19.11 In cities and towns where the Muslim community share a cultural heritage, converts tend to accept Islam from the cultural perspective of the community concerned. One participant mentioned the acculturation that occurs, for example, when a convert has become Muslim through Arab or Pakistani contacts. The more the convert adopts the traits of the Arab or Pakistani culture the higher the degree of acceptance she is likely to experience within Arab or Pakistani communities. Without adopting the cultural interpretation of Islam as defined by the host community, the convert is not considered to be a proper Muslim. She may in fact be regarded as an individual who is ignorant or badly informed.

19.12 At the same time the convert may become increasingly less accepted by her family of origin who become alienated from the convert as her behaviour and dress differ increasingly from their cultural norms and values. The price the convert pays frequently is the loss or suppression of her own ethnic or cultural identity. The acceptance of the conversion by family and friends is rarely straightforward and is frequently viewed as incomprehensible and something that changes the person in a detrimental way.[52]

19.13 For converts joining *Salafi*-orientated groups, attempts to remove all ethnic/cultural aspects from the practice of Islam were viewed to be inherent to *Salafism* which seeks to offer 'pure forms' of Islam untainted by cultural accretions and racism. This search for 'pure forms' of Islam were considered unrealistic and unattainable by several of the participants. *Salafi* groups offer converts a place where they are welcomed into established Muslim communities but where acceptance is predicated on assuming somewhat dry, and often prescriptive interpretations of Islam. These may become increasingly difficult to assume as the convert develops their own knowledge and understanding of the different ways in which Islam can be interpreted and practised.

19.14 While some converts form an allegiance to *Salafism*, for many others it becomes a stage they go through before moving on to experience other expressions of Islam. At times *Salafism* attracts converts because of the stark contrast it offers to British culture. It may appeal to particular people who seek certainty and a dichotomised view of the world, and where a Muslim can be defined as much by what they oppose as with what they accept.

19.15 Many female converts are attracted to Islam because they want to feel secure and protected from the sexualisation endemic in Western culture.[53] Part of the justification of Muslims seeking a pure, reified form of Islam is the protection and seclusion of women. This may lead to a schism between progressive and 'pure' forms of Islam, and may result in the progressives going so far as to lose Islam and the purists seeking retrograde, stultifying interpretations of the faith. One participant mentioned how the *fiqh* of Islam has always been amenable to change and adaptable to local customs. She cited the example of Imam Shafi, (a theologian whose work constitutes one of the four major schools of Islamic law in Sunni Islam) who changed his understanding of aspects of *fiqh* after moving a few hundred miles within Egypt. 'Here we are over 1000 years later, still thinking we need the same *fiqh* that has been propounded for the last 1400 years; we need to question this'. Participants felt that the Muslim community needs to raise the level of the teaching of traditional knowledge, using modern teaching methods. 'There is a need to push the boundaries gently.' One participant argued that converts need to raise debates about how Islam has developed. 'Are we seeking to replicate the Islam of 7th Century Arabia, or do we derive morals and principles which transcend time and space?' the same participant asked.

The urban experience of Islam

19.16 Islam in Britain today is primarily an urban phenomenon, with the vast majority of Muslims settled in the major cities of the UK. Seventy-four per cent of Muslims in the UK are of South Asian heritage. Thirty-eight per cent of all Muslims in Britain reside within five London boroughs. Despite an educated professional class of Muslims operating at all levels of British society, the majority of Muslims are located in highly concentrated, deprived inner-city areas, often in geographically segregated, ghettoised Muslim communities. Thirty-one per cent of working age Muslim men are economically inactive, as are 69% of working age Muslim women.[54] Muslims constitute 4.8% (2.7 million) of the UK population while Muslim youth constitute 21% of the young offenders' prison population.[55] Given that this is the constituent base of Muslims in the UK, participants questioned the extent to which heritage Muslims were in a position to offer help and support to converts, and to what extent the expectations that converts held of the heritage Muslim communities were realistic. It appeared that the responsibilities may lie in the opposite direction, with converts needing to assist ailing heritage Muslim communities.

19.17 Converts frequently experienced exclusion in their attempts to penetrate tightly knit South Asian communities which demonstrate strong cultural influences in their interpretations of Islam. It was noted that insularity is part of the experience of being a migrant minority, living in what is perceived by some Muslim communities to be a hostile, alien culture. The example of British expatriates residing in Spain who band together in tightly knit British enclaves, recreating a British cultural lifestyle in another country, was cited to illustrate that such behaviour is a common feature of immigrant communities.

19.18 Throughout the discussions on intra-Muslim relations participants commented on the great extent to which interrelationships and engagement between different Muslim communities are absent. Heritage Muslims appear to operate largely within their own ethnic enclaves. Pakistanis have their own organisations and polarised communities, as do Bengalis, Arabs and other Muslim ethnic groups. Communities are constituted along sectarian and ethnic lines, with little (it seems) cross-fertilization. Mosques and mosque committees in South Asian communities are constructed along tribal lines which serve to exclude tribal outsiders, not just converts. 'The mosques of Bradford are not reaching out for the convert experience', one participant felt. Nevertheless, the converts' lack of tribal allegiance was often considered helpful in this context, because what they contribute stems from their status as individuals from outside a particular Muslim community.

19.19 Mosque committees are generally formed of men in their sixties. While some male converts have assumed positions of authority on mosque committees, it is generally acknowledged that even this is the exception rather than the rule. One participant stated 'my gender barely gets me through the door, and because I don't speak the language, there is no way I am going to get on a mosque committee'. In contrast, Prophet Muhammad said, 'do not deny women their share in the mosque'. This statement underpins a period in history when women actively participated in the promulgation of Islam and were engaged at all levels of Islamic society.

19.20 Serious issues regarding the lack of engagement of convert women in the communities and organisations in which they live may be due in part to a marked lack of self-confidence. A number of participants mentioned that they are reticent to express their knowledge for fear of being berated by heritage Muslims. Converts are commonly not regarded as knowledgeable about the practice of Islam by many heritage Muslims, who feel the need to challenge their practice of the faith. One participant stated, 'I researched how to pray, how to do *wudu* (ritual ablution). Because I raised my hands at different times to him, my brother-in-law told his kids to ignore the way I do my prayers, 'she's English, she does it funny'...not a possibility in his eyes that he is the one that's doing it wrong'. She added: 'I have been Muslim longer than some of the kids in the youth centre have been alive, and they still think that because I am White my experience of Islam is deficient to theirs. I still doubt myself. I have been Muslim for over a decade, then someone will say something about *sira* (the life of the Prophet and his Companions), then I will think maybe I don't want to embarrass myself, I will go away and find out that I was right.'[56]

19.21 One participant described how of all the heritage Muslims she has come into contact with, the most difficult to interact with are the self-consciously secularised, who have 'liberated themselves from Islam.' This participant found that the ways in which she practised Islam were belittled by this group. Wearing a scarf was viewed as an embarrassing, retrograde step that was not welcomed in the social circles of the educated elite, who felt they were tarnished by associating with her.

20. Identity

20.1 Participants considered it essential that converts actively seek to create positive representations of Islam, and themselves. Frequently, identity is created in the negative. Instead of forging identity in this mode, it was argued that a positive, self-generated view of identity be promoted by Muslims for whom faith stands for peace, justice and for ethical standards in private and public life, a point which needs to be more widely conveyed to the British public. One participant noted that the rise of a confident, inclusive identity is slowly emerging within Muslim convert communities. The growing number of converts in the UK will possibly enable this to happen as a larger community of converts emerges.

20.2 It may take generations to create a British Muslim identity, something that is both authentically British and authentically Islamic. It was noted that within eighty years of the *Hijra*,[57] pagoda-style mosques in China were built. These did not reflect the style of mosques built in Medina, but were a physical manifestation of the interpretation of Islam prevalent in China, infused with Chinese culture. Participants noted that today globalisation may make it harder to construct distinct indigenous identities because of the wide range of global influences which impact the perception of identity.

20.3 Converts thought it necessary to be able to express their Islamic faith within a framework reflective of British cultural values and assumptions, in the same way that a Pakistani, Bengali or Arab community is infused with their cultural norms. Converts should not feel that their values must be neutralised in order for Islam to be practised. It could be argued that in a culture where Islam is the dominant faith its cultural practices are likely to be more deeply reflective of Islamic ideals than those of a Western society such as Britain. For example, hospitality towards guests in Muslim societies is integral to cultural expectations and is inextricably linked to both the culture and to Islam. In contrast, a convert to Islam brought up in Britain would have to acquire the knowledge of the Islamic etiquette of how to be appropriately hospitable to guests.

20.4 The group felt that converts should not be made to feel uncomfortable about their cultural background, (nor consider it inferior) in order to be accepted by heritage Muslims, nor should their cultural background be perceived as a threat to heritage Muslims. For one British-born (White) participant, the attempt to reconcile her activities across a range of different cultural milieus made her feel as though she had a split personality. At home she socialised only with Arabs but outside she mixed with people from a range of other cultural backgrounds.

20.5 The validity of the concerns of heritage Muslim communities was considered in relation to the threats to values and ways of life which they perceive to be posed by British culture. To mitigate this, it was suggested that converts express awareness that their interpretation of Islam should not be lauded over that of heritage Muslims. They might acknowledge that heritage Muslims may have adopted an apparently insular, introspective frame of mind in order to protect themselves from religiously-inspired racism and bigotry displayed towards them by wider society. Moreover, converts of African-Caribbean heritage may find that the racism they experience from heritage Muslim communities is more endemic and entrenched than that expressed by wider British society. One participant of African-Caribbean heritage maintained that the 'way our communities bonded together may appear exclusive, but reflects the fact that the biggest disappointment we have faced has been with other Muslims.'

20.6 For female converts in particular, the challenges of dealing with institutional structures such as mosques and Islamic organisations that exclude female participation may result in women creating alternative structures to address needs and issues of concern. Alternatively, Muslim women, including female converts, may decide to be more proactive, and to push for more access into organisations and institutions. Debates may be structured around exclusivity and lack of organisational access. One participant asked: 'Why do we allow women to be discriminated against in the mosques? Why are we not pushing for women and the disabled to have equal access to the mosques? Women have fought for centuries for rights, so why do we allow men to take away those rights?'

20.7 Disquiet was expressed by the participants over organisations that were perceived to be failing converts. The accusations levelled against these organisations included an inability to acknowledge who the convert was, where she had come from and the needs of her family. Participants' comments included the following. 'I want organisations to be inclusive of my needs and those of my family.' 'My Dad was not ready for the fact that I became a Muslim and died before we could be reconciled. So I feel that if after 30 years you are not ready for me to walk into your mosque, for you to work actively as an organisation... then how do we deal with organisations that are failing us?' The *darul ulooms* (Muslim-style seminaries) are producing dozens of women trained in Islamic theology. However, there was no way of assessing what type of contribution these women are making to improve the life of Muslim communities, and to what extent they are able or equipped to address the challenges convert women face.

20.8 One participant believed that converts should broaden their parameters to include the needs of non-Muslims when developing organisations. Another considered that where mainstream non-Muslim organisations were already established, Muslims should be accessing services from them, and should not need to establish parallel organisations, designed specifically for Muslims.

20.9 Participants raised issues of whether to evolve a strategy allowing convert women to engage with heritage Muslim communities, or whether convert-only sub-sections, or organisational structures should be pursued. For some heritage Muslims, a strong specific Islamic-convert identity might appear threatening and challenging to their notions of how Islam should be manifested in Britain. To some heritage Muslims aspects of 'British Islam' may smack of reified governmental interference and external attempts to influence discourse on expressions of Islam in the UK.

20.10 The participants disagreed over the composition and need for convert-only organisations or forums. One participant who supported the need for convert community organisations argued that they were required to address the unique issues and concerns facing converts, which are best addressed by converts themselves. Attitudes will not be changed on an individual basis she said, but require a coherent response by individuals and organisations representing converts. Overall, however, the desire was not to establish enclaves of converts, but to participate within wider Muslim community organisations.

20.11 There was recognition that convert support network organisations need to be openly inclusive, and reflective of, the multi-cultural composition of the UK's convert population. This would necessitate lobbying at both local and national levels to raise the provision of services, and the access to decision-making forums in order to provide responses focused on a range of sources of help and assistance to converts.

20.12 The comments of younger participants provided insights into their positive experiences of inclusion. 'The young Muslims I have encountered have accepted me, although I have witnessed, but not experienced, exclusion.' One participant cautioned against being part of a closed group, but advocated actively mixing widely with Muslims. She reiterated the need to be wary about who converts involve themselves with, because as a 'recent convert you are susceptible and impressionable, and you don't possess the knowledge that enables discernment. Over time, you learn to distinguish between culture and Islam.' Another stated 'I have had many opportunities to travel, both within the UK and the United States, and my journeys have been facilitated via local [Muslim] networks in each area.'

20.13 Other participants reiterated that change was occurring for the better and that improvements could be seen. The young have more opportunities. Nevertheless, the UK was considered to be behind many Muslim countries, where access to mosques was readily available to women and a lack of segregation was apparent. In the UK, unnecessary restrictions were placed on Muslims, in pursuit of some reified form of Islam.

20.14 In order to make Islam accessible to Muslims from all walks of life and open to the wider British public, it was suggested that the central mosques of each city should be designed to offer amenities such as those provided by the central mosque of Dublin, which houses amongst the prayer facilities a gym, meeting room, funeral facilities and a restaurant, open to all the community, not just Muslims. Some British mosques are moving in this direction but they remain a minority.

20.15 Discussion ensued over the extent to which a convert who comes to understand the belief systems and cultural norms of both Muslims and non-Muslims can become a bridge across the cultural divide. The metaphor of converts as a 'bridge' between two disparate communities (Muslim and non-Muslim) was frequently alluded to in the symposia. One participant voiced her concern that if converts act as bridges, then converts are keeping communities apart; what is needed is to cross the bridge. Another participant stated that the problem with being a bridge was that people tend to trample on you. There was a desire to build links between communities, develop networks between people and foster a sense of belonging.

20.16 It was unresolved how far connections can extend into the Muslim communities, without bridges being burnt with the family and friends that the convert leaves behind. One participant mentioned that she was constantly building bridges with her family, only to have international events involving Muslims constantly fracturing those bridges. There were questions over the extent to which individual converts possess the skill to cross cultural divides, both within Muslim communities and across multi-faith intercultural ones. It was felt in the context of the latter, that converts are often pushed forward to enter into discussions with other faiths, particularly Christianity, to effect discredit on the others' views. This necessitated that converts be careful and sensitive about how they present themselves and their conversion narratives

20.17 It was felt that engagement with the arts enables increased intra-Muslim and inter-cultural contact to develop. There is a growing interest and participation in Islamic arts and fashion, although this remains small-scale and isolated. Coordination will be required for artistic endeavours to have a meaningful impact on the wider Muslim communities. Cross-cultural art groups reflect the multi-cultural influences that constitute the composition of Islam in Britain.

21. Media

21.1 Since the inception of Islam, forms of media have been used to discredit it. At the time of Prophet Muhammad, poetry was a major weapon in this enterprise. Quraysh, the Prophet's own tribe, wrote poetry against Muhammad and Islam to incite hatred against the faith. To counteract this defamation of the faith, the Prophet commissioned one of his companions to write verses of poetry in defence of Islam. The modern situation reveals that little has changed over time, and that there is still a pressing need for people who can counteract the largely negative media coverage of Islam.

Research involving Islam commissioned by the Mayor of London revealed that in any given week 91% of stories about Muslims presented negative portrayals, using emotive, abusive and inflammatory language, with terrorism being a major theme.[58] In spite of this, the best media coverage in Europe concerning Islam was considered to be in the UK. Organisations such as the Muslim Public Affairs Committee, UK monitor representation of Muslims in the media, and lobbies to redress negative coverage.[59]

21.2 Participants discussed media representations of converts, which varied from respectful and fascinated interest to distorted characterisations of conversions. Converts serve to confound and challenge racist, stereotypical and negative narratives of heritage Muslims, because their culture and heritage is inherently British in nature.[60] As an indication of the type of coverage that converts may receive, one participant cited a piece she had seen in a broadsheet newspaper which asked, 'what sort of woman freely converts to a religion which supports the oppression and torment and murder of thousands of Christians, homosexuals and spirited women worldwide every year! The sort of woman who writes letters to a serial killer!'

21.3 Converts are often seen to be rejecting British values by the media because British people are not commonly Muslim. 'She used to be British but now she is Muslim' seems to be a prevailing attitude when talking about convert women. There is apparently a general incomprehension as to how British people could wish to become Muslim. While conversion to Islam happens in a number of ways to very different people, media interest in conversion has largely focused on White, educated, middle class women. These conversions cause shock and consternation, due to the assumption that educated women are giving up a liberated lifestyle to accept a way of life that is poorly understood by the British public. In this context, one participant observed that Caribbean people are not connected with Islam in people's imagination. Their conversions are silent and invisible. Some participants thought that the it was not in the media's interest to discuss Black conversion to Islam. The media, she commented, is not interested in portraying African-Caribbean conversion stories and does not want to encourage Black conversions, which are seen as a threat to the status quo.

21.4 Frequently the media focus has been on the external appearance of White, middle class converts. Choice of dress attracts particular interest. The adoption of a headscarf moves the convert from being a member of this group, to being an outsider or foreigner. The media wish to speak to headscarf-wearing converts, to someone who looks visibly Muslim and has a Muslim name. 'Do you wear a scarf?' is commonly asked of converts when being approached for an interview. One convert with dual-heritage background was contacted by a well-known broadcasting service and a daily newspaper for interviews on her conversion to Islam. When they discovered she was half Asian they were not interested in her conversion story. This she considered was due to her mere status 'as a convert going from one foreign thing to another foreign thing.'[61]

The impact of negative media coverage and Islamophobia

21.5 Participants argued that the impact of the daily drip feed of negativity focusing on converts and young Muslims that emanates from the media is damaging and difficult to deal with. Indirect messages imply that Muslims do not belong in this country; one participant said: 'it took me a long time to deal with it.'

21.6 Unwarranted attention from strangers was perceived to be disturbing. One participant recalled three hostile incidents when out in public. She recalled one particular incident when a woman shouted, 'nice bag luv, got a bomb in that?' when she was carrying a rucksack in central London. Another incident involved being called a terrorist. It appeared that even young children are influenced by the negative portrayal of Muslims. A little boy in a seaside resort, on seeing a convert, asked his parents 'are Muslims our friends?'

21.7 The media at times dismiss conversion to Islam as evidence of the strange personality of the convert. A participant mentioned a film screened on television entitled 'White Girl'. This was a portrayal of a White girl from a dysfunctional, poverty-stricken family, seeking sanctuary from the harshness of her family life through her conversion to Islam. Here, the portrayal of the convert was as someone impressionable, vulnerable and emotional. Islam is not viewed as a valid extension of the values that many British converts have grown up with. Another example was cited of a young girl who had an anti-social behaviour order (ASBO) imposed upon her. Islam became a positive force for improvement in her behaviour following her conversion. However, this could equally be construed negatively, as an example of her extreme character, to go from an alcohol-drinking girl with an ASBO to a convert to Islam.

21.8 The '*War on Terror*' declared by the United States and its allies in response to the events of 9/11 shifted the media presentation of Muslims from the 'Other' to the 'dangerous Other,' serving to further demonise the faith. Media representations commonly portray Islam as monolithic, and no account is taken of the many different representations of Islam that are present in Britain.[62]

21.9 A popular theme in newspapers is the clash of cultures, where Muslims are perceived to be imposing their world view on British society, threatening its values, culture and traditions. Presentations of an 'us and them' dichotomy serve to distance Muslims from British values and norms of behaviour. For example, a tabloid newspaper considered the lack of labelling of *halal* meat as a risk to British people in that they might eat *halal* hamburgers and therefore practice Islam without knowing it.[63] Such coverage encourages the crude portrayal of a global clash of civilisations. Muslims are perceived as bad, foreign and not British and the idea that Islam is against the West continues to be perceived as a political reality. In reaction, Muslims respond with an 'ambivalent discourse of hubris and defensiveness'.[64]

21.10 There are very few media stories presenting Muslims as unproblematic, never mind worthwhile, members of British society. The good positive behaviour displayed by the majority of the Muslim population is rarely newsworthy. Converts involved in terrorism make news. The demonisation of Muslims in the mainstream media is a recent phenomenon, not prevalent in 1960's Britain. Today, the terminology connected to Muslims in the media very often includes words such as 'terrorism', 'fanatics', 'extremists', 'violent fundamentalists', 'backwards', 'medieval' and 'anti-civilisation'.[65] A 2010 YouGov Poll revealed that 58% of the population associated Islam with extremism and 69% with the oppression of women, while only 6% associated Islam with justice.[66]

21.11 Extremist detractors of Islam often discussed converts to Islam in radical terms, assessing their propensity to engage in terrorist-related activities. Here, an alarmist portrayal presented White converts as particularly dangerous because they can slip through security at airports without being detected as Muslims. Recent newspaper reports may have unwittingly contributed to alarm within the media, by emphasising unreliably high estimates of the number of converts considered to be residing in Britain, thought to be in the region of 100,000, serving to heighten public concern.[67]

21.12 One participant thought that converts were considered fair game for attacks, owing to their choice of Islam as a faith. Whereas being Jewish was regarded as being part of a race, albeit a diverse race including blonde White European Jews and Black African Jews, being Muslim is seen purely as a choice. Participants recounted comments such as the 'only good Muslim is a non-practising Muslim who does not wear *hijab*, drinks alcohol and does not pray frequently' – i.e. has eliminated their unacceptable 'Otherness' to mainstream society. One participant commented that Muslims have inflicted this 'Otherness' on themselves to an extent that seems to justify the English Defence League's position that they are not racist but are against Islam as an alien religion.' Another participant saw groups such as the English Defence League as a cover for general expressions of prejudice and hatred.

21.13 'Becoming Muslim challenges the secularisation of our society', one participant felt. 'Secularism has come to mean anti-faith and pro-rationalism. If you choose faith you are irrational and not credible.' It was considered that Muslims are frequently guilty of imposing narrow and simplistic cultural understandings onto British society and almost invite ridicule from the press. This was exemplified for one participant by the actions of a University Islamic Society which lobbied for one of the toilets to be converted into a squatting one.

21.14 One participant commented, 'it is not that we are not Christian that surprises people, it is that we are religious enough to affect the way we behave, the way we dress and that we pray five times a day'. Buddhism is seen as a private choice whereas Islam is viewed as a political identity.

21.15 One participant mentioned how aggrieved her non-Muslim mother was at the amount of negative media representations of Muslims, especially with regard to how little it bore relation to any of the Muslims she had met. She acknowledged it was hard for non-Muslims to know where to position themselves given the media representations of Muslims as opposed to the actual examples of the Muslims they came into contact with.

Counteracting negative media coverage

21.16 Participants argued that effective engagement with all forms of media would help to counteract the negative coverage of converts to Islam. However, one participant expressed her reluctance to engage with the media in case the media retaliated with a smear campaign against her, which could damage her career prospects and chances of marriage. Another convert cited the example of an inter-faith singing group who were infiltrated by a sinister man connected to the media with a range of organisations that are not friendly to Islam. This situation required intervention from the police. This example was considered to be a warning to be cautious when dealing with the media. In spite of this, it was considered necessary to engage with the media in order to ensure that moderate voices were heard. Otherwise radical proponents of Islam would be promoted as the sole representatives of all Muslims.

21.17 Most participants agreed that converts should not be afraid to express their identity and opinions, and to 'take Islam with them wherever they go'. It was thought imperative to emphasise the shared values among Islam, Christianity, Judaism and other faith traditions. Some Islamic values are European values. Converts must not entertain the quiescent mentality of some heritage Muslims by succumbing to pressures to remain silent in the face of unfair criticism.

21.18 Positive media coverage was considered possible. Muslims can contribute to campaigns and stand up against what is wrong in society. Converts can use the media to highlight the truth about Islam. One participant cited the well-known *hadith* in which the Prophet is reported to have said: 'If one of you sees something wrong, let him change it with his hand; if he cannot, then with his tongue; if he cannot, then with his heart and this is the weakest faith'.[68] This *hadith* challenges Muslims to take some form of action when confronted by unacceptable things regardless of who the target may be.

21.19 Examples were given of powerful lobbying groups who have in some cases been successful in generating debate but may have at the same time stifled criticism. It was thought unwise to emulate groups that had succeeded in closing down debates.[69] It was considered essential to encourage discussion about Islam and ensure that eloquent people are available to effectively represent Islamic opinion. Opportunities are available for converts to take effective forms of action and to counter the negativity emanating from the media on a daily basis. These could include making phone calls, writing emails, or arranging mosque open days so that the media is not the only source of information about Islam for non-Muslims. Here, the purpose would be not to convert people to a certain point of view but to offer them the opportunity to consider alternative perspectives, allowing them to make up their own minds. Converts need to consider how positive messages can be disseminated about Islam.

21.20 Out of largely negative media coverage, some positive aspects have emerged. Focus on Islam by the media has served to spark interest in Islam, which has led some people to research further into the faith and leading in some cases to conversions to Islam. One participant said 'the media was a big source of my learning – it didn't put me off'.[70] Converts may reach out to non-Muslims and seek to inform and educate them about Islam, perhaps in ways different to heritage Muslims. Converts have better insight into how to communicate with non-Muslims because they were previously non-Muslims. However, many Muslims will not accept this. One participant felt that 'converts should be more vocal and speak out and stop this victim mentality. I understand that Muslims feel victimised, but we have to lobby for ethics in journalism. I've written a novel [unpublished] about being a Muslim to show what Islam can be like.' Another participant mentioned the positive relationship she had established with the BBC. Converts also needed to be aware that the media is not just making news, but reflecting what is going on in society. We 'need to be aware of what they expect and then bust it with love and respect', one said.

22. Citizenship, political identity and engagement

22.1 The extent to which non-Muslims and heritage Muslims may accept the identity of converts as Muslims will vary according to the individuals and the communities with which the convert comes into contact, as well as how acceptable the particular narrative of conversion is perceived to be. For converts, identity is a fluid and continuous process of self-evaluation and re-evaluation aligned with the possibilities of arriving at a comfortable sense of Self. Generally, conversion entails more of a widening of identity than an emptying out of a previous identity. For some converts, the problems posed by presenting a unified identity mean that multiple identities are adopted to facilitate interaction with a variety of social, cultural, political or religious milieus. This can lead to a chameleon effect, where the convert is constantly adjusting their self-presentation to suit changing interactions with different types of people, groups or cultural or religious situations. In this way they may not be able to be true to their own perception of how they wish to present their identity or may remain unsure of who they are or who they want to be. Other converts, stronger in their sense of Self, are able to comfortably express a more resilient sense of identity regardless of the social setting in which they find themselves.

22.2 When addressing political identity, a participant commented that some converts are 'completely crazy' with regard to the self-presentation of who they are. This can involve an outright and extreme rejection of the UK and who they were prior to their conversion. Readjusting identity can make some converts susceptible to the multiple and conflicting identities offered to them by different representations of Islam as adopted by heritage Muslim communities. It is common for converts to go through periods of uncertainty and confusion regarding what it is to be a Muslim and how to become the kind of Muslim that a convert desires to be. Trying to fit in with other Muslims may involve adopting positions that a convert is not entirely comfortable with or which are at odds with previously held beliefs. One participant felt that both Muslims and non-Muslims attempted to impose an identity on her, effectively telling her 'this is how you are to dress, think and feel' in an attempt to either distance her from Islam or her British identity. She described the effect on her as one of 'giving her a split personality.'

22.3 For a dual-heritage participant the decision to embrace Islam involved a shift from being a member of a largely accepted minority to becoming part of a religious minority that attracts intensive scrutiny over what it represents. Before conversion she had felt accepted and British. Following conversion she felt as though she had become part of a minority – entering a different social category which shifted her relationship with the state. 'I questioned my values and what I stood for,' she said.

22.4 Converts and heritage Muslims in Britain perceive a need to demonstrate allegiance to British culture and values which may not be required of other minority groups in the UK. Heritage Muslims, in particular, are seen as not sufficiently grounded in the UK, leading them to question the extent to which Islamic values accord with European values. There is a perceived need amongst Muslims to prove their European-ness.

22.5 There are very specific challenges for Muslims and the state. Muslims have particular experiences of citizenship which can at times feel not quite typically British. There is a prevalent idea in Britain that Muslims embody interests that are foreign rather than British. Political leaders must partly take responsibility for creating a climate of mistrust around Muslims in Britain by linking them to terrorism or by unfairly accusing them of not wanting to integrate into British society.

22.6 The participants felt that the three major British political parties appear to be increasingly estranged from the specific political concerns of religiously-orientated British Muslims. This may lead to Muslim disengagement from the mainstream body of politics. In the domestic sphere there is a struggle to involve Muslims in the process of policy formulation. Traditional political Muslim allegiances to the Labour party have been irrevocably damaged by the pursuit of foreign policies targeting Muslim populations abroad. This sense of political disenfranchisement will not be healed until the Muslim voice is seen as a resource to be utilised in the development of foreign policy.

22.7 Participation in party politics was debated in the symposia. Some participants favoured direct involvement in political parties in order to effect change from within, while others considered engagement in politics to be problematic. A convert may be unwittingly co-opted into the political system without being able to produce any tangible changes in policy formulation. Converts may also find themselves caught in the middle of irreconcilable differences between the aspirations of their co-religionists and those of their families, leading to extremely stressful situations at a time when they may in fact be extremely vulnerable on all fronts. Some participants were also concerned that participation in politics may make them appear to be malleable to government influence which is perceived to be in favour of a quietest form of Islam. The participants agreed that politics matters, but it is not for the faint-hearted.

22.8 Converts are often involved in Islamic organisations that represent political issues of direct concern to members of the convert and heritage Muslim communities. There has not, to date, been any reports of contemporary converts taking on the mantle of religious-political involvement, following the example of the high-profile Victorian converts Abdullah Quilliam and Lord Headley who had influence in the highest echelons of British society.[71]

22.9 It is difficult to find suitable representatives for Islam. One participant was disparaging about some of the convert organisations currently in existence: 'some of the most horrendous people I know were (from) convert organisations', she said. Progressive leaders and scholars sometimes raise themselves to the level of celebrities, posturing and becoming unavailable.

22.10 Conversion to Islam does appear to affect the political outlook of converts. Those who have little political awareness prior to conversion may become awakened to the issues that are affecting Muslims in Britain and other parts of the world. 'Becoming a Muslim sharpens your perception of what really goes on in the world, including the plight of women'. There was also a growing realisation of related political issues such as the environment, fair trade and ethics. However, this political awakening is not without problems. While remaining sympathetic to the issues surrounding Muslim communities, several converts expressed exasperation at being expected to assume the mantle of representatives of these communities or of being expected to express an allegiance to extraneous political causes often located in tribal or regional quarrels. A non-British participant stated: 'I am not British – these issues are Bangladeshi issues – or issues that have nothing to do with me. Regarding issues of ethnic politics, why as a convert, should I be exposed to moral pressure to adopt issues that are related to politics and not to Islam?'

22.11 One participant mentioned the pressure on her to become a spokesperson for Palestinian causes because, as a Muslim, she was considered by non-Muslims to be an authoritative voice on such issues. Another was asked to discuss forced marriages which she considered to be 'horrible and need to be addressed – but these are not my issues.' This discussion raised the issue of whether there was a moral imperative on the convert to adopt political causes that pertain to heritage Muslim communities. Opinions were divided. Some felt that the moral nature of these issues makes them human issues rather than Muslim ones. In this sense, they deserve to be championed by converts. Others felt that converts have enough concerns on their plate which merit attention first before they can turn to the issues affecting the countries of origin of heritage Muslim communities.

22.12 Converts remain largely outside of the ethnic politics that engage sectors of the heritage Muslim communities. Political votes for candidates in the UK can be secured *en bloc* through the communities settled in British cities, based on tribal allegiances in ancestral villages in the South Asian sub-continent. This situation constitutes a barrier to those converts wishing to engage in domestic politics from a faith perspective. Converts wishing to assume public office would have to negotiate the quagmire of these allegiances if they were seeking to represent a constituency with a Muslim population.

22.13 Participants discussed the extent to which government policies are precluding political engagement by Muslims. The conservative practices of some Muslims are increasingly regarded in Britain as anti-social and as potential precursors to violent radicalisation. In response it was argued that the values underlying these practices are not so different from those adhered to in 1940's and 1950's Britain.[72] In spite of this, there are increasing fears amongst Muslims of being labelled as 'extremist' or 'terrorist' because of their adherence to these values.[73] Such labels are unlikely to be applied to non-Muslims holding similar views. The prevalence of widespread Islamophobia exhibited by sections of the British population also serves to curtail political involvement.

22.14 The dual identities of British converts mean that there is potential for them to play an important role in society. According to one participant, their contributions 'cannot be ignored when considering the challenges posed by the Far Right and religious extremists.' Converts often possess an acute awareness of how Muslims are perceived by the wider non-Muslim society. Educated converts can distinguish between Islamic ideals and the cultural practice of Muslims; this makes them able to 'to present a balanced view of Islam and Muslims that might be accepted by the majority society.' However, the vulnerability that often comes with conversion may reduce the ability of convert women to immerse themselves in politics. This may be seen to confirm the stereotype of Muslim women as politically disengaged, subjugated and, as one participant put it, 'not entirely worthy of the many rights that accrue from social, economic and political participation in society.' The secular nature of politics in Britain was cited by some participants as a reason for thinking twice before they immerse themselves in political activity.

22.15 Secularism was not considered a barrier by some participants, arguing that it is wrong to equate it with atheism. These participants argued that Western political ideals are consistent with Islamic values. The 'Inspired by Muhammad' campaign designed to educate non-Muslims about Islam, highlights the many points of convergence between Islamic and Western values.[74] A number of participants acknowledged that the West is currently better at implementing values such as justice, human rights and social care than Muslim-majority countries. As the Prophet relied on non-Muslims as guides to get him from one place to another, so it was argued that Muslims should take the best from what is offered by the West to build their own institutions and organisations in a manner that is consistent with Islam.

22.16 Participants noted with regret the failure of Muslims to adequately address problems arising from the cultural misappropriation of Islamic ideals and rulings. It was necessary to utilise the British legal system to ensure that rights were upheld. 'British justice will give you your Islamic rights,' commented one participant; 'Islamic practice can be found under non-Islamic law, more so in fact than is practiced by heritage Muslims,' another participant added.

23. Women's rights

23.1 Several of the participants espoused a political awareness which they had come to through an Islamic reworking of Western feminism. For one participant Western forms of feminism had initially held negative connotations, conjuring up for her images of unkempt women. However, after being introduced to the writings of feminists who were Muslim, she revised her perceptions. Feminism was perceived by several participants as inseparable from equality. However, one participant commented: 'I believe in equality but that doesn't mean I am a feminist.' It was acknowledged that there was a lack of recognition and awareness of feminist Muslim writers amongst Muslims generally and little understanding of feminism in its historical context.

23.2 The need to raise the status of women within Muslim communities was generally acknowledged. One participant noted that a woman entering the Muslim community following conversion can experience an apparent demotion of status. Her general observations had led her to conclude, 'we suffer from misogyny and discrimination administered by Muslim men. They talk and what they say is law. I am used to debating on an equal footing. What jihadists and Islamists say becomes the new gospel for some converts and members of the heritage Muslim community.'

23.3 Participants were widely critical of *Sharia* Councils/courts operating in Britain, which were considered to discriminate against women's Islamic rights. Some participants described them as 'mickey mouse courts' based on 7th century interpretations of Islamic law. Concern was expressed regarding the capabilities of those accorded the authority to make rulings in a fair and just manner, given the often narrow and dogmatic interpretations of Islam that are perpetuated by religious scholars, especially as these have been proven to be detrimental to women's rights as enshrined in Islam. One participant commented that raising awareness of issues such as forced marriages and securing the necessary assistance to counter this practice was more likely to be achieved through non-Muslim British courts. Muslim women would be better advised to seek justice through these courts than those applying *Sharia*.

24. Guidance and spirituality

24.1 Some participants thought that heritage Muslims frequently give misleading and misguided information to new Muslims. One participant cited the case of her sister who no longer practised Islam after being fed misinformation. Several of the participants expressed an awareness of the dangers of not keeping good company. They argued that converts are vulnerable and need to be aware of whom they are associating with. This included groups of Muslims whose influence on converts will encourage them to make radical changes to their lifestyles and beliefs. One participant expressed concern over converts whose understanding of Islam was limited and who appear to have complex problems to deal with, which may include mental health issues, or adoption by radical groups. Here, such converts were insufficiently aware of the problematic nature of the particular interpretation of Islam offered to them, making them potentially susceptible to manipulation and radicalisation.

24.2 Concern was expressed regarding the lack of access to spiritual teachings. It was recognised that many *Salafi*-orientated groups had the means to disseminate their ideas much more easily amongst Muslim communities. Emphasis from the *Salafi* groups was often placed on determining who was Muslim and who was not, and this was perceived as harmful and divisive by the participants. These groups provide mosques and services which are open and welcoming to converts, providing them with acceptance and a sense of belonging to a Muslim community. Converts can be susceptible to being drawn into *Salafist* interpretations of Islam, without necessarily having an understanding of broader and different perspectives regarding the ways in which Islam can be practiced.[75]

24.3 The lack of support from the heritage Muslim communities and other more established converts is exacerbated for female converts, who do not have access to the religious infrastructure that converts to other faiths enjoy. There are few courses of instruction in the rudiments of the Islamic faith. Many mosques and Islamic organisations remain inaccessible to women, which make it difficult for female converts to meet and engage with other Muslim women, as well as to participate in community life.

24.4 In terms of educating converts about Islam, women who had married heritage Muslim men recognised that frequently husbands played a key role in guiding their convert wives. One participant's husband, although from a heritage background, lacked knowledge about Islam and so they had grown and developed together in terms of gaining insight into Islam.

24.5 One participant mentioned the role that her adult son played in guiding her understanding of Islam. He had achieved a respected role within their local Muslim community and his mother remained aware that her behaviour must not jeopardise his standing or reputation. Such influence is not always benevolent and a participant cited the example of a friend whose four sons dictate her life choices. Other participants mentioned a reticence and timidity on the part of converts in expressing opinions on Islam or in exhibiting forms of behaviour that may elicit disapproval from other Muslims. There was an awareness of the need not to threaten conservative elements, which could result in being ostracised by members of heritage Muslim communities.

24.6 A number of the participants had sought the guidance of sheikhs from Sufi *tariqas*[76] and had taken *bay'a*[77] with them. For some, this had involved travelling extensively across the Muslim world in order to find spiritual guidance. On aligning themselves with a spiritual guide, they accorded a high degree of personal agency to their sheikh, who provided them with a direction for their lives and for their practice of Islam. This relinquishment of personal autonomy included accepting the sheikh's advice on where to live, what job to take and who to marry.

24.7 One participant considered that access to higher spiritual states could be achieved through active citizenship and that time and energy devoted to spiritual endeavours should be balanced with engagement in practical good work. This implied that an excessive immersion in spiritual practices could appear self-indulgent and lead a convert to neglect collecting the great rewards gained from service to humanity.

24.8 Some participants did not favour the use of sheikhs as spiritual guides in favour of a personal expression of spirituality. In these cases spirituality involved an appreciation of communal prayer and time spent in the company of good people. In this context, one participant noted the damage done to the soul by spending time with non-Muslims, 'whose conversations would veer towards subjects that are painful to listen to and damaged their sense of peace and focus on God'.

24.9 A relationship with the Qur'an provided a very spiritual and moving experience. One participant described that when she was reading the Qur'an she felt like 'God was addressing [her] personally'. She had been introduced to mosques which offered dry and legalistic perspectives on Islam and had subsequently moved beyond this to incorporate spiritual practices into her life that added 'critical substance' to her faith.

24.10 Converts were frequently called upon to provide guidance to non-Muslims who had developed an interest in Islam. This sometimes proved problematic when the person presented themselves as clearly troubled and possessed dubious motivations for conversion. This led to the dilemma of whether to advocate conversion when aware of the further problems this might create for a person not able to address problematic issues generally, never mind any additional ones created by conversion.

24.11 Issues were also raised, although not fully addressed, regarding how scholarship can be used to control converts. It was acknowledged that the development of the convert occurs over time and as knowledge of the faith increases, so does the ability to make an intellectual assessment and evaluate information that is being presented, including distinguishing between cultural interpretations of Islam and Islam itself. In the initial stages of conversion a convert is likely to be confused by the array of conflicting advice that she receives, especially when it is infused with any cultural bias that distorts Islamic precepts.

24.12 Mosques have always been at the heart of Muslim communities throughout the Muslim world. In the UK, where some mosques prevent women from attending prayers, a major route into the Muslim community is effectively curtailed. The participants noted that the mosques they had attended were often dirty and offered women cramped conditions in which to pray, disconnected from the main prayer halls used by men, and without a view of the Imam leading the prayers. Some of the participants did not attend the mosques, primarily because they refused to be made to enter through the women's entrance and to pray in a dusty basement. The solution offered was to create mosques controlled by converts but open to the wider Muslim communities, where converts can have access to services and facilities that are specific to their needs.

25. Sufism

25.1 Participants discussed the extent to which Sufism is accessible to converts and is able to provide them with a comfortable avenue to express their Islamic beliefs. *Sufism* or *tasawwuf*, as it is known in Arabic, describes an inner mystical dimension of Islam through which practitioners seek to draw closer to the Divine. This is commonly achieved through 'esoteric' practices, asceticism and *dhikr*.[78] Other interpretations of Islam contain mystical dimensions, but these are expressed with a different emphasis. There are many forms of *Sufism* that embody a divergent range of beliefs and practices. It is to these *Sufi* orders that many Western converts are particularly attracted.

25.2 Most of the *tariqa*s found throughout the Muslim world also have followers within the UK.[79] While some *tariqa*s are based in mosques, others with less formal structures may appear more welcoming to converts, for instance, ones where meetings take place in members' homes. In this sense, the *tariqa*s subvert the formal structures of the mosques, which are said to present too many barriers for convert women to overcome.

25.3 Because Sufi meetings are often less institutionally bound, issues can arise for converts over how to access information about the *tariqa*s, such as who organises them, where they are held and what beliefs they propound. Converts tend to explore a range of different *tariqa*s before they choose the one with which they are in tune spiritually. Again, as with *Salafism*, some converts will find a comfortable place within a particular order, while for other converts *Sufism* becomes an encounter from which they move on. One participant argued that the strong influence of *Salafism* that converts frequently encounter has pushed the *tariqa*s underground, because people are reluctant to admit to their involvement with *Sufism*. The South Asian *Barelvi*[80] form of Sufism with its strong links to caste and *pirs*[81] remains an impenetrable structure to converts, to which they are unlikely to have access.[82]

25.4 One participant considered that *Sufism* has the ability to spread out into communities and that it readily adapts to local customs.[83] Its often gentle approach to Islam may prove appealing to many converts who are seeking a place where they feel comfortable with the presentation of Islam and can find acceptance. The participant described a multicultural *tariqa* which had offered a supportive environment to converts, who assumed positions of leadership within it and found social benefits such as networking, links to employment and assistance with housing. Another participant mentioned that the *tariqa* she attended had become her 'lifeline'. This gave her access to a spiritual path and training where links with like-minded people could be formed—-sharing an intellectual and spiritual focus, providing spiritual nourishment and strengthening her faith.

25.5 Another participant who had visited *Chishti*[84] *tariqa*s in India disagreed. She found that the *tariqa*s in the UK were 'culturally-bounded and their doors are closed to Black women'. It was felt that *tariqa*s should be the forum for people to share spiritually-bounded values, but that this often fails to materialise because people get caught up in issues focused on culture. 'Islam should be our common value; if it's not Islam what is it?' the participant asked. Black people, she maintained, were treated differently than those of other ethnicities within the *tariqa*s in Britain.

25.6 Converts would frequently travel widely in their search for spirituality and to further a deeper understanding of God. It was not uncommon for converts seeking spiritual truths to travel to countries such as Morocco, where the warmth and welcome they found there enabled them to develop their faith as Muslims. One participant mentioned that 'the Qur'an states that we should call ourselves Muslim, but we are on a journey to become true believers.' Sufi *tariqa*s provide that journey.

26. Imams and scholars

26.1 Acknowledgement was made regarding the necessity to train Imams who are equipped to recognise and address the needs of converts, and who possess an in-depth understanding of British society. It was agreed that enlightened Imams could come from any country, and that it was not essential to adopt a parochial approach which insisted on only British-born Imams and scholars leading Muslims within the UK. A prerequisite was that Imams have a good command of the English language. For many Muslims, the first point of call regarding any issue concerning Islam is the Imam.

26.2 Scholars and those offering theological advice needed to be able to offer relevant guidance and solutions to pressing social questions. Muslims, and converts in particular, should be asking vigorous questions of scholars so that they can develop relevant solutions to pressing issues that are significant to their co-religionists in Britain.

26.3 Throughout the history of Islam, the greatest theologians and thinkers have been those who have offered controversial opinions and were frequently derided as heretics. It was felt that today scholars appear to go for softer options and shy away from offering contentious or divisive views. Converts and Muslims generally are equally guilty of choosing safe options. Thus, when Imams make the practice of Islam more difficult or complicated, Muslims gravitate towards these modes of thinking because there are commonly held assumptions that the harder course must more accurately reflect the correct *sunna*.[85]

27. Struggles within the faith

27.1 Several participants described their relationship with Islam in the following ways. 'Islam is a coat that many people have to put on and take off many times, and the coat is my journey into Islam. As long as I have God I have Islam. To make me forget God is the only way I can leave Islam.' Another participant commented that the process of developing faith involved 'question, doubt, confidence and then doubt again.' She added: 'I know there is a living God and I am on a journey to be the most perfect example of what it is to be human. I am still on that journey.'

27.2 For those new to Islam, there is a struggle to gain understanding of what Islam is. One participant described her gravitation towards Islam as that of feeling 'compelled to do something that is very strange, yet, you know you must do it'. Another commented: 'God would not have selected us to be Muslims if He was intending to leave us alone. We arrive at our own authentic understanding of what Islam means to us.' She added: 'We are – all too often – seen as freaks who have made an incomprehensible choice that might be explained away as eccentricity: the insincere by-product of a marriage, the outcome of psychological crisis or disorder, social maladaptation or naive sympathy for the latest form of Third World-ism. All these common stereotypes are largely the outcome of a thoroughly secular worldview that sees religion as the irrational, superstitious 'Other' to itself, and it must, therefore, explain away any serious religious commitment as a cipher for some personal or political discontent.'[86]

27.3 Tests of faith for converts were presented in many forms. Detrimental experiences with heritage Muslims were one type of onerous test. Outlined here were the dangers of manipulation. One participant detailed how after hearing of a sheikh on television she had attended his meetings. There, she discovered the five daily prayers, along with fraud, emotional manipulation and vicious racism. 'It was a betrayal of my trust', she said. Other converts involved in that group were equally traumatised. She gave the example of one, whose father had attempted to extricate him from the group by having him taken to a remote location with a team of brainwashing experts, who tried without success to de-programme him. The son had been promised by this Sheikh that he would lead England into the golden age of righteousness behind the *Mahdi*, conditional on a lot of money being donated to the group.[87] The level of exploitation was so high that his father disowned him and he was disinherited from an extremely large estate. Such an example described the vulnerable condition of naïve converts, who have failed to understand what their faith entailed and are, as a result, subject to exploitation. Other converts can be encouraged to join a group without being aware of it as a political movement with a radical agenda.

27.4 One participant found a lot of 'idiotic disinformation' targeted at converts. Most young people are finding information about Islam from the Internet and from friends, and not from the mosques. Embracing Islam was 'still a journey of the determined', to know what to avoid, and to apply some intelligence from the beginning. 'The easy thing when you are on this journey is to adopt the costume'. By this was meant that the external vestiges of Islam are adopted without understanding their internal effects and impact on the heart. 'This wonderful thing of *hijab* is becoming a poisoned chalice. Is the *hijab* wearing you or are you wearing the *hijab*?' one participant asked.

Doubts about the faith

27.5 Some Participants asked: if life is about choices and a choice is made that served to eliminate all other choices, what would be the outcome? A perceived lack of exit points may frighten someone considering entering Islam; this may ultimately serve to deter them from entering the faith. It is widely believed that it is not possible to renounce the decision to adopt the Islamic faith. Some converts express concerns about what would happen to them if they decided to leave the faith and be considered an apostate, leaving aside the fear about going to hell. The point was expressed that apostasy and the related death sentence in Islamic law were considered to apply to traitors, actively plotting against the state, and not to a person who no longer wished to actively adhere to Islam.

27.6 Doubt in itself was seen as an important thing, helping individuals to consider, question and evaluate decisions taken. Participants considered what things would constitute disillusionment with Islam, and might lead them to consider abandoning their faith. Adopting Islam was considered by one participant as fundamentally alien to where converts had come from. For some participants, trying to practice Islam became a form of pressure – 'people give the opinion that there is no flexibility'. Muslims become disillusioned because they cannot see how to live an Islamic lifestyle in modern-day Britain. For others pressures were found in the belief that adherence to certain norms was compulsory to be within the bounds of Islam. Converts need to be able to progress at their own pace, but other people, generally heritage Muslims, may not allow that to happen.

27.7 One participant who had negative experiences of the heritage Muslim communities, considered that those guided to Islam by books and scholars will inevitably come to feel let down. She considered that while one is searching for something positive, the hypocrisy and behaviour of other Muslims will be disturbing. Being guided by one's inner Self was discussed as a suitable approach. This method had led one participant to some profound spiritual experiences.

27.8 Doubts had led one participant to question the very essence of her faith. She had asked herself, 'what is right with this religion?' and had come to the tentative conclusion that very little was. Resolving such disquiet had led her to the consideration that spirituality was not an adherence to a faith or religion, but a state of being. 'I would not call myself a Muslim, except in response to a direct question... Now I just find the establishment of this religion or the establishment of any religion just does my head in. I'll never go to (a) mosque again.'

27.9 Others felt that being Muslim constituted being part of a community. Participants questioned, 'who has the right to tell you where you should be?' One participant considered that she could not say if she would leave Islam, 'I didn't even want to be here, I don't know how I got here, so who I am to predict what is going to happen to me?'

Disappointment with scholars and sources of knowledge

27.10 The participants shared difficulties that they had experienced in accepting opinions and interpretations offered by scholars which were often less than relevant to the complexities of life in contemporary Britain. Knowledge needed to be embedded within the context of contemporary life. A participant mentioned that it was the individual responsibility of all converts to study and increase their own knowledge; the lack of relevant scholarship cannot be blamed 'on an imaginary group of people'. If scholarship cannot be trusted, converts needed to engage in their own research.

27.11 One participant mentioned that she had had numerous teachers before finding a suitable one. She had not found any through mosques. She found that there were scholars who would quietly take the time to answer questions. It takes converts time to realise that many people will not have the capacity to answer questions. 'You need to find your own answers; they will have their own answers, you need to find yours.' Advice was reiterated by the participants to take counsel, but to think independently. Frequently, traditional answers are given and most people are not sufficiently critically aware to be able to evaluate the credibility of advice. All the answers you may discover are within the range of possible answers to a question. It was important to be able to make a moral choice that you can account for in front of God.

27.12 It was generally acknowledged that once an opinion or comment was presented to converts it often established a niggling doubt in their minds as to the extent of its truth. While one participant questioned the extent to which converts actually believe what they are being told, another commented that when being presented with an opinion which goes against what is rationally believed by a convert, there is still the temptation to think it is 'probably right: I'm just not good enough to accept it.' The question was how to empower converts so that they have the confidence, based on sound knowledge of Islam, to be able to effectively challenge and counteract what they perceive to be inaccurate or misleading counsel.

27.13 One participant believed that an individual accessed Islam through her intelligence. Questioning authority and scholarship was considered possible, while acknowledging that within traditional scholarship there is a lot of truth. A humble attitude is required to understand the truth. Understanding takes effort, and a person's understanding can be wrong, although Islam cannot be wrong. Scholarship provides an array of answers which require judgement to determine which one(s) to accept. Scholarship cannot be accorded the status of the word of God. Questions arose as to how to gain access to a scholar – 'they are so far removed from us.' It was pointed out that where dilemmas needed to be addressed, the possession of innate resources could be drawn upon, such as reliance on the *fitra*, the inner guide, the instinct within, which allows for the development of the natural spiritual Self.

27.14 Many reasons for leaving or retreating from Islam were outlined. A participant said that she had met a number of people who had left Islam due to husbands who treated them badly; some of these former converts express contempt for the Muslim communities they had known. Others fail to relate to the books on Islam available to them. Another participant described meeting heritage Muslims, who themselves had left Islam, being unable to cope with the cultural straitjacket, the fire and brimstone version of Islam, and who had found themselves rebelling against narrow-minded interpretations of the faith. A convert couple were mentioned who had left Islam because they could not relate to the heritage Muslim community.

27.15 Another participant mentioned that she would only leave Islam if she found a more authentic belief system. She had chosen Islam because she thought there was truth in it, while acknowledging that the packaging of religion is produced by people. This has led her to take a step back from organised religion with no desire to be involved in organised events. Her's was a need to focus on connecting to God in a meaningful way. 'I haven't been doing all my prayers and would sometimes rather sit in bed and have a meaningful communication with God, rather than doing all those physical motions ...(which are to me personally) not always meaningful.'

27.16 One participant had many unanswered questions about Islam to which she hoped to find the answers. When discussing her faith with Muslim colleagues at work, she was accused of adopting innovative, unsanctioned practices (*bid'a*) which were directing her to follow the government's line on Islam, whereby politicians were attempting to mould passive Muslims. She asserted that by becoming Muslim, she had chosen a moderate path. 'Sometimes at night, I feel like an absolute psychopath. I go to sleep at night and would like to connect with God and pray *Isha* (the final of the five obligatory daily prayers) but I just want to go to sleep. People will tell me I am letting *Shaitan* (Satan) influence me. I am really confused, but if I admit this to other people, they will think I am coming off the path (leaving Islam).'

27.17 Most people enter the faith on a spiritual high, the point at which commitment is propelled by intense spirituality. They are then berated by people, telling them all the things they are doing are wrong – this, for one participant, was the point at which she might have considered leaving Islam. Taking into account the variations in personal strength, where there is minimal community support, some converts may consider it better to leave Islam. For others, the faith does not root itself deeply into the soul. Some converts find spiritual groups or their teachings actually lead them away from the faith.

27.18 One participant noted that some converts experience a diminishing loss of sense of Self – becoming a shell of their former Self, and feeling empty inside. It was noted that when a heritage Muslim keeps a low profile nobody passes any comment, but for a convert to do the same is seen as evidence that their faith is waning, or that they may even be thinking of leaving Islam. If a convert disappears from their local mosque or study circle it is as if they have left Islam. This was seen as 'the '*kafir*' blood still pumping in the convert's veins, enticing one away from Islam.

27.19 One participant outlined how, when she first became a Muslim, she was very much on her own and everything was fine until she met the Muslim community. Her first visit was to a mosque, which she did not enter, because she refused to go through the side door. She commented, 'It was put across that if I don't accept this I was not Muslim. So I avoided the mosque for two years. I struggled between my faith and the community. I did think about leaving Islam: the fundamentals of the faith kept me in.'

27.20 Some of the inadequate rulings directed at converts may have profound implications for their attitude towards the faith. Converts have been advised that attending the funeral of a non-Muslim parent or relative would put them outside Islam. Women who are married to non-Muslim men and then convert to Islam have been told that it is impermissible to remain married to their non-Muslim husbands. This is all ill-advised as Islam did not come to destroy families or to break up marriages. In order to clarify previous misinterpretations a *fatwa* had to be issued by the Islamic Council of Europe insisting that a woman in such a situation does not have to leave her husband. This highlights the need to constantly challenge unacceptable rulings that are being promoted. Despite the issuance of such *fatwas* they remain largely obscured or deliberately concealed from the mainstream body of opinion.

27.21 One participant was told it was not acceptable to be married to her non-Muslim husband following her conversion to Islam. Partially influenced by this advice, and compounded by existing problems within the marriage, she divorced her husband and became a single parent. This convert is now experiencing profound difficulties in finding people prepared to facilitate introductions to enable her to consider remarriage. She considered that divorcing her husband was a necessary sacrifice she needed to make as a means of making herself more Islamic. It was thought that such damaging advice could impel some converts to choose to abandon Islam. Similarly, there is no way of determining the extent to which experiences of bad marriages propel women into abandoning their faith. While there are attempts to estimate the number of converts coming into Islam, there are no similar attempts, at present, to estimate the numbers of those who have left the faith.

27.22 Another participant mentioned that her path to Islam had been facilitated by the way she had been parented and her mother's handling of Christian religious tradition. No scholarship or books were involved in her conversion. Subsequently, when raising her own children, her teaching came from the heart. She expressed this by saying that 'If scholars are saying something and my heart is screaming out this cannot be so, I trust my heart first and then with my head I research. I trust myself first.' 'Treat scholars like plumbers, ask for three quotes (*fatwa*s),' she added.

The effect of Islamophobia on retaining faith

27.23 Being a Muslim in a contemporary society infused with Islamophobia is a difficult choice to make. The pervasive influence of Islamophobia can deter people from becoming involved with Islam, while for others its very denigration can lead to inquisitiveness and inquiry, of wanting to know more about the faith. For one participant, 'everything that everyone thinks is so bad is something I want to know about.' Her inquisitiveness about Islam had led to her eventual acceptance of the faith.

27.24 For many Muslim women their visibility as Muslims, displayed through the adoption of the headscarf and forms of modest dress may increase the likelihood that they experience Islamophobic reactions from non-Muslims.

27.25 For one participant, wearing a headscarf was part of the close bond that she shared with other Muslim women. To another participant, the headscarf constituted a red flag that induced Islamophobia in non-Muslims. The *hijab* is not an absolute thing with an absolute value – it is very much an individual experience in the way that it can make the journey into Islam much harder. One participant who did not wear a headscarf thought that this enabled her to challenge people's preconceptions about Muslims. People were able to engage with her, rather than being immediately confronted with her religious beliefs. She considered that 'if the *hijab* (headscarf) did not come with all these instantaneous judgements, applied by people, maybe I would have chosen to wear it.' She found it easier not to have to deal with all the baggage that is associated with wearing a scarf and quite liked it when people eventually found out about her faith. Here, her faith was practised privately and within the spheres that she felt comfortable with. 'I don't want my religion to become every aspect of me. I think that would be the aspect that would drive me away from Islam – the pressure.' It was acknowledged that drawing attention to oneself could become a source of pressure and impact the experience of being Muslim by hindering the process of developing faith.

27.26 The participants listened to the experiences of another participant who did not adopt the headscarf, but still felt the full impact of Islamophobia when she lost her job as a direct result of her conversion to Islam. The participant felt she had been dressed in a virtual *hijab*, because, mentally, people apply mental forms of dress to a person even though they are not wearing the clothing concerned. Islamophobic attitudes had led to her being ostracised from the social circles in which she moved. This made her re-evaluate her friendships, but not her faith.

27.27 For converts who are not married and, therefore, lack family or community support, or who live in isolated areas devoid of Muslims, it was thought that experiences of Islamophobia would be harder to deal with. Being part of a Muslim community was considered to be a source of strength that could provide the impetus to be positive even when not actually with other Muslims.

27.28 Another participant who had an ambiguous relationship with the headscarf, which she wore on particular occasions, argued that it is wrongly viewed as 'the flag of Islam.' She considered that Muslim women could find more imaginative ways to cover their heads than to wear a headscarf – something would sit more comfortably within the culture in which they live, for example, a hat. Since male converts, generally, dress in a manner similar to the rest of the male population, their faith is not readily apparent through their dress. Another participant mentioned that when her husband entered a plane in a suit this did not elicit any reaction from passengers. However, as a *hijab* wearing woman, she felt she was considered to be a terrorist with a bomb in a rucksack, although she did not want to be the cause of fear or alarm for non-Muslim passengers. While Muslim women may decide not to wear a headscarf due to concerns over their potential safety, or not wanting to declare their religious affiliation openly, there is also an inherent danger of internalising the perceived prejudices that other people may hold and, thereby, reinforcing Islamophobic attitudes almost in a self-imposed way.

27.29 Another participant admitted to harbouring actual feelings of Islamophobia herself after being deeply disturbed by terrorist attacks in London: '[non-Muslims] see us with blood on our faces. I am Muslim, I love Islam and I am Islamophobic.' She found it traumatic to sit next to a brown person on the tube in possession of a rucksack without wondering whether she should get out at the next stop.[88] In this case, Muslims were being constructed as the 'dangerous Other' by other Muslims, along with assumptions that it was necessary to deflect moral responsibility and the blame for the behaviour of unknown people to whom there was no connection apart from a shared faith. The Muslim world, blighted by corruption and despotic leadership, was similarly viewed as disgraceful. When people go on an anti-Islamic rant, the participant agreed with them: 'When you see people with faces of hate in Trafalgar Square, saying 'behead all Christians,' I feel sorry for them. They might say they are carrying the flag of Islam, but they are not. The Prophet would disown them.'

28. Concluding remarks

28.1 The participants attending the symposia debated complex issues in a frank and open manner. They were willing to discuss private issues in a way that, to the best knowledge of the project team, had not been discussed before in a collective meeting. This environment of trust and openness was a tribute to the project organisers who had created a safe space in which discussions could take place. This meant that dissenting voices were expressed without creating discord among the participants. The effective chairing of the symposia by the Project Leader, which injected balanced summaries into the debates, played a major role in the success of this project.

28.2 The participants found the symposia very useful. For many they proved to be a cathartic experience, almost a form of group counselling or therapy. The narratives of conversion contained both humour and sadness. Experiences were shared and this led to an empathetic exchange of issues of concern. The symposia allowed for networking to develop old friendships and establish new ones.

28.3 The speakers leading the symposia gave insightful perspectives on the issues under discussion and were able to frame the subsequent debates with considered opinion. However, the symposia sometimes moved at the level of generalities because of the complexity of the issues they invoked or the lack of settled perspectives in some cases.

28.4 The symposia elicited the struggles that are part of the conversion experience in specific areas of faith, politics, gender, identity and sexuality. Here lay explorations of how to navigate such areas from perspectives that are acceptable to the converts, and which sit comfortably with their own understanding of how they want or expect Islam to be a part of their lives. This involves an examination of the extent to which Islam becomes the dominant element in their lives and whether their experience of living Islam is one that is all-encompassing or compartmentalised.

28.5 The symposia elicited tensions between the converts and the heritage

Muslim communities. In part, this is due to cultural differences in attitudes and expectations regarding faith, gender, sexuality and politics. Such differences overshadow Islamic ideals and may be the result of an inability to allow teaching to traverse historical time frames and geographical settings.

28.6 For many converts, attempting to navigate heritage Muslim communities means adopting more conservative perspectives on life, and inculcating attitudes that may not sit comfortably with those they have grown up with—-which may be more relaxed, nuanced and less judgemental. While there are many valid criticisms of aspects of heritage Muslim communities, there was collective acknowledgement of the input of those same communities into British society and their efforts to establish systems of mosques and Islamic organisations and facilities across the whole of the UK. Most converts in their initial stages of conversion will have met individual heritage Muslims who have attempted to assist them through their conversion and enabled them to become part of existing Muslim communities. A lack of acknowledgement of the positive elements of the heritage Muslim communities would constitute a considerable disservice both to the converts, for failing to recognise this, and to the heritage Muslims themselves for the help they have been able to provide.

28.7 Where poor or misleading information is offered, this is often attributable to the convert going to the wrong sources for advice. While it is acknowledged that a convert may not be aware of who to approach for advice or where to access appropriate written material, there is a responsibility on both the heritage and convert Muslim communities to offer appropriate guidance and assistance where possible. Just as one would not approach the Islamophobic English Defence League for advice on community cohesion, neither would one expect to receive enlightened advice on Islam from non-mainstream Islamic organisations that project unorthodox views. The vulnerabilities that comprise the convert experience are the responsibility of both converts and heritage Muslims to address, and neither should abdicate the responsibility of improving the lives of those who have chosen Islam.

28.8 While problems, issues and concerns were discussed, the participants also considered ways in which the converts could develop a sense of community and the necessary steps to address the lack of services required to help them cope with the challenges they face. Such suggestions could provide the basis for developing strategies designed to improve and overcome many of the problems commonly faced by converts. For improvements in the situation of converts to occur, converts themselves need to be prepared to do more than voice their opinions. Transformation of the environment within which converts engage demands that converts actively participate in bringing change and reform to fruition.

29. Recommendations

1. Community and Political Engagement

- Raising the profile of the convert community to enable them to become more proactive within heritage Muslim communities, particularly through volunteering in mosques, Islamic organisations and other community initiatives.

- Developing awareness of the positive impact that Islam can play within British culture through training and encouraging converts to re-engage with community, social and political initiatives that benefit the whole of British society.

2. Counteracting Racism and Islamophobia

- Raising awareness of the heritage of African Caribbean Muslims and their significant contribution to the propagation of Islam through scholarship and spirituality. This must be an important theme in historical and contemporary analyses of the broader appreciation of the Islamic heritage to the wider global society.

- Developing strategies to challenge effectively media misrepresentations and Islamophobic attitudes in British society through full, active participation and engagement.

- Building awareness within the convert community on how to engage effectively with the media to counteract stereotypical and negative narratives of Islam and Muslims.

3. Mosques

- Mobilising the convert community to utilise existing structures within mosques and Islamic organisations to extend the provision of facilities and services specific to the needs of this community. Such services must be designed and delivered with the input of experienced and mature converts who should form part of the governing bodies of the institutions concerned.

- Establishing training programmes to improve the pastoral care offered by Imams to the convert community.

- Mobilising the entire Muslim community to facilitate the presentation of mosques in a clean, welcoming and holistic manner where the needs of Muslims are accommodated.

4. Marriage

- Developing marriage services that explore the steps that can be taken to protect the interests of converts including providing advice where required.

- Creating a rigorous pre- and post- marriage advice and counselling support services.

- Training and developing a guardianship structure that ensures the rights of women are upheld and secured with marriage contracts playing a major role in safeguarding the rights of both men and women.

5. Education and Training

- Devising a list of reputable and knowledgeable male and female scholars that converts can consult, who understand the range of issues and experiences that affect converts. This will help to counteract ossified interpretations of Islam and aid its contextualisation in Britain, with English being used as a common language to aid inclusivity.

- Developing strategies and structures to facilitate scholarship amongst female converts, along with effective training programmes for women, to enable them to participate at governance and organisational levels within the community.

- Developing courses nationwide to instruct converts and heritage Muslims in the beliefs of Islam and to assist in the understanding of the development of different interpretations of the faith as they are represented in Britain.

- Providing comfortable and secure forums for converts to meet together and discuss issues of concern pertaining to matters of interest arising from the conversion experience, including issues of gender and sexuality which merit special consideration.

6. Social and Cultural opportunities

- Developing, with the involvement of converts, a range of social activities to engage the Muslim communities in the cultural and historic heritage that is part of contemporary Britain in order to foster better relations and appreciation of the society in which they live.

- Developing arts, music and culture in order to provide avenues for creative interests and expression.

7. Counselling and Advice Services

- Developing an infrastructure for the convert community that is focused entirely on the growing range of services required to meet the needs of this expanding community.

- Developing confidence-building training for converts.

- Offering counselling for emotional and personal issues, including advice on effective ways of presenting Islam to converts' families.

- Exploring the needs of support networks already in existence throughout the major towns and cities across the UK to build the necessary resources to assist these networks in continuing to develop and deliver their work.

- Developing a system of referrals to existing social networks and services, and establishing services designed to provide for the specific cultural and religious needs of converts.

- Ensuring that women converts are aware of their rights as citizens under British law and, if considering marriage to a heritage Muslim, impressing upon them the importance of having a deeper cultural awareness of the community to which he belongs.

Appendices

Appendix One

QUESTIONS: SYMPOSIUM I

Family, Appearing as a Muslim & Lifestyle

1.1: Family

- Who guides and how guidance is provided to those expressing an interest in Islam?
- At what stage in the conversion process do converts present their interest in Islam to their families and how is this achieved? How does the convert respond to the reactions from family members?
- To what extent does marriage impact upon converts' understanding, implementation and expression of Islam?
- How can a *fiqh* of minorities be applied to converts and what would be the perceived benefits of doing so?
- To what extent do cultural expressions transposed upon Islam and transmitted to converts contribute to the breakdown/straining of family relationships between converts and their families of origin?

1.2: Appearing as a Muslim

- How far do outward expressions of Islam convey change within a person? Is there a link between dress and piety? Does dress have an impact upon spirituality?
- How significant is spirituality in the conversion transition and the continuing conversion process? To what extent does research address the importance of spirituality in conversion?
- To what extent can an assessment be made of the social impact of appearances both to Muslim and non-Muslim society?
- How do converts counter the insecurities arising from expressing or not expressing Islam through dress codes?
- What are the possible effects of changing names/identities?

1.3: Lifestyle

- How do conversions to Islam impact upon converts' lifestyles? What changes do they initiate?
- To what extent are British modes of socialising compatible with a converts' new beliefs and life style?
- Is compromise involved when maintaining relationships with non-Muslims? How?
- How do converts re-socialise themselves within the non-Muslim majority communities? To what extent are they able to achieve this?
- What, if any, roles should converts play in order to create better understanding/relations in society between Muslims and non-Muslims? What are their chances of success?

Appendix Two

QUESTIONS: SYMPOSIUM II

Intra-Muslim Relations, Marriage & Media

2.1: Intra-Muslim Relations

- How do converts maintain a distinct presence among the heritage Muslim community? To what extent are they accepted as authentic Muslims? What are the barriers to inclusion?
- To what extent do heritage Muslims question the converts' interpretation or practice of Islam? What impact does this have on the notion of 'believing as ourselves'?
- Is there any evidence to suggest that heritage Muslims and Islamic organisations want to maintain a degree of domination and control over converts?
- How do anti-Western sentiments held by elements of the heritage Muslim communities impact on the convert's understanding of citizenship?
- How do converts negotiate an unfamiliar religious infrastructure, particularly one that is perceived as not designed for heritage Muslim women or female converts?
- With theology derived solely from Muslim countries, how can theological approaches develop to incorporate Islam in a British context so that scholars can respond appropriately to issues of concern and the needs of converts that are specific to the UK?
- Do converts make a conscious choice to adopt Shia, Sunni, Ismaili or other interpretations of Islam?
- To what extent do converts move between sufi, *salafi*, Deobandi, Brelvi or other interpretations of Islam that are found among the heritage Muslim community?

2.2: Marriage and forms of marriage

- How are marriages organised for converts? Who facilitates marriages for converts? Can converts facilitate their own marriages successfully?

- Where can converts find support and assistance both before and during marriage?
- Does the lack of family and community support impact on the converts' marriage experience? How?
- How do the children of converts to Islam fare in Muslim communities and non-Muslim majority communities? What impact does their parents' conversion make on their future decisions regarding their religious faith? How does this conversion affect their ability to integrate into British society and their life chances?
- Are there differences in experiences according to whether one or both parents are converts, where one parent is born into the faith and the other is a convert or, if the parents convert during different stages of the child's life?
- To what extent can polygyny be accepted in a Western context?

2.3: Media

- How do media representations affect converts self-perceptions and how do they influence the views of wider society?
- Does the media promote representations of converts as radicals, potential or actual terrorists and, as such, anti-Western?
- In the mixture of 'curious fascination and incomprehension' that influence the media portrayal of conversion, what aspects of conversion are emphasised and which aspects fail to be acknowledged through media outlets?
- What can converts do to challenge Islamophobia or media hype about Islam and Muslims?
- To what extent are relationships between converts to Islam and heritage Muslims portrayed by the media as deviant or culturally inappropriate?
- How do the media deal with the rate of conversion to Islam in the UK?

Appendix Three

QUESTIONS: SYMPOSIUM III

Genders and Sexuality, Identity, Citizenship and Political Engagement & Struggles within the Faith

3.1: Gender and Sexuality

3.1.1 Gender
- Can a Western view of gender coexist with the Islamic faith?
- Does conversion to Islam necessitate a re-evaluation of a convert's attitude towards gender equality?
- Does conversion provide a form of empowerment or a form of oppression for the female convert?
- How does the process of conversion affect the way women are viewed by the non-Muslim community?
- Does the experience of being a Muslim woman differ from what you think Islam offers women?
- How do converts perceive the representation of Muslim women by their own (convert community) and the heritage Muslim community?
- Some members of the heritage Muslim communities may possess misogynistic attitudes towards women which are not only based on double standards, but also operate against the tenets of Islam. How do these views impact on female converts?
- Does a female convert have a more difficult experience in conversion than a male convert?

3.1.2 Sexuality
- How do notions of the norms of Western sexual activity impact on female converts?
- To what extent do attitudes towards female sexuality affect intimacy within marriage?
- In a society which places so much emphasis on a woman's attractiveness, does opting out of this social trend empower or disempower her?
- How has the process of conversion impacted your views on sexual orientation?

- How should British Muslims deal with lesbian, gay, bisexual and transsexual converts to Islam?
- Does a distinction between acts and beliefs enable a more tolerant and compassionate approach to LGBTs?

3.2: Identity, citizenship and political engagement

3.2.1 Identity
- How do converts present their identity as Muslims?
- Do converts experience immediate full acceptance of their identities when they come into Islam?
- Conversely, do converts feel pressured to compromise their cultural identity when they come into Islam?
- Does a convert have to empty out some of their existing Western identity when converting?
- If so, does this hollowing out of an identity make them susceptible to multiple and conflicting identity pressures presented by Muslim communities?

3.2.2 Citizenship and Political Engagement
- Does conversion affect a convert's interaction or relationship with the state (the ability to be politically, civically or locally engaged or their political leanings)?
- Does conversion change the types of role a convert can play in their local communities or in national politics?
- Where accepted norms held by wider society conflict with Islamic values, how does a convert respond to these?
- Is it difficult for a convert to engage with the community or state as a 'representative' of the Muslim community? How?
- With far-right politics being ever more focused on Muslims, do converts find themselves more, or less, politically active or aware after conversion?
- How does a convert experience politics within the Muslim community?
- To what extent are converts under pressure to accept conservative or even extremist political views, for example, those which hold that political engagement in a non-Muslim society is a form of impiety?

3.3 Struggles within the faith

- What facets of Islam do converts find difficult to reconcile with their previously held beliefs?
- How do converts maintain their faith and what difficulties may cause their faith to waver?
- How difficult is it to differentiate between the behaviour of Muslims and Islam?
- Is leaving Islam an option or even possible? Why?
- Do people remain as Muslims because of the perceived penalties associated with leaving Islam?
- Questioning Islam – is this possible?
- To what extent does the rise of Islamic fundamentalism and Islamophobia contribute to converts wishing to leave Islam?
- Can gender differences and the notions of control and authority as perceived by male Muslims be a contributory factor to converts leaving Islam?

Notes

[1] Female converts report that it is easier to wear the *hijab* in big urban centres such as London, Birmingham or Glasgow than in small cities, town or villages. Big urban centres afford the female convert more anonymity and, therefore, more freedom to display outward signs of her faith, should she choose to do so, through the *hijab*.

[2] White British female converts in the project reported being asked where they came from in spite of their looks and indigenous British accents. When they answered that they were from Manchester, London, Glasgow, Newcastle (and so on), they were then told 'yes, I know, but where did you come from before you came to Britain?' According to this response, a person may cease to be authentically and originally British, suggesting that for the respondents Islam is an 'alien' category in the British imaginary. This view is starkly captured by the following comment in the report, in reference to White female converts,: 'She used to be British but she is Muslim now.'

[3] The cover picture of this report has been chosen to reflect the contrast between visibility and invisibility that I am discussing here.

[4] The assumption underlying this term is that the original state of being (*fitra*) is submission to God, and this meaning is encapsulated in the term 'Islam'. For this reason, so-called conversion is nothing but re-version, and no Muslim can be a New Muslim. The term 'heritage Muslim' is a description that is culturally and socially, not doctrinally, bound.

[5] Some participants queried how accurate it was to call converts 'new' when some of them have in fact been Muslim longer than some heritage Muslims have lived.

[6] Strictly speaking, polygamy is the practise of having more than wife or husband at the same time. Polygyny refers to the practice of having more than one *wife* at the same time.

[7] The Prevent strategy, launched in 2007, 'seeks to stop people becoming terrorists or supporting terrorism. It is the preventative strand of the government's counter-terrorism strategy, CONTEST'. http://www.homeoffice.gov.uk/counter-terrorism/review-of-prevent-strategy/.

[8] Pbuh: 'Peace be upon him' is the formula used by Muslims when referring to Prophet Muhammad. It is assumed that this formula is implied in all references to the Prophet when his name is mentioned in this report.

[9] 'Convert', *OED*, 2012, http://www.oed.com/.

[10] Ibid.

[11] 'Revert', *OED*, 2012, http://www.oed.com/.

[12] 'Turk'. *OED*, 2012, http://www.oed.com/: 'Often used as: = Muslim…to turn Turk'. 'Turk' was used to generally describe those living in Central Asia and held to be pejorative.

[13] Estimates vary as to the number of British converts to Islam in the UK. Brice (2010) considers there to be somewhere around 100,000 British converts, calculated using data extrapolated from the 2001 census. He also estimates that conversion is occurring on a 2:1 ratio of females to males. Brice, K., (2010), '*A Minority Within A Minority: A Report on Converts to Islam in the United Kingdom*', Faith Matters. http://faith-matters.org/images/stories/fm-reports/a-minority-within-a-minority-a-report-on-converts-to-islam-in-the-uk.pdf

[14] Some parents may compare their child's conversion to Islam favourably against engagement with negative activities such as crime and drugs. Participants considered that this does not necessarily reflect a less pejorative view of Islam on the part of such parents, although it could be seen as such in certain circumstances.

[15] Zebiri (2007) notes three categories of family responses to conversion which range from outright

acceptance to acceptance over time, to long term estrangement and rejection. Zebiri, K, (2007), *British Muslim Converts: Choosing Alternative Lives*, Oneworld Publications: Oxford.

[16] Islamophobia is a form of religiously animated racism. The Runnymede Trust (1997) identifies eight components that define Islamophobia: '1) Islam is a monolithic bloc, static and unresponsive to change. 2) Islam is separate and 'Other.' It does not have values in common with other cultures, is not affected by them and does not influence them. 3) Islam is inferior to the West, being perceived as barbaric, irrational, primitive and sexist. 4) Islam is violent, aggressive, threatening, and supportive of terrorism and engaged in a 'clash of civilizations'. 5) Islam is a political ideology and is used for political or military advantage. 6) Criticism made of the West by Muslims is rejected out of hand. 7) Hostility towards Islam is used to justify discriminatory practices towards Muslims and exclusion of Muslims from mainstream society. 8) Anti-Muslim hostility is natural or normal.' The Runnymede Trust, (1997), *Islamophobia: A Challenge For Us All: Report of the Runnymede Trust Commission on British Muslims and Islamophobia*
http://www.runnymedetrust.org/uploads/publications/pdfs/islamophobia.pdf.

[17] Zebiri and Joseph, in Zebiri, (2007), p105.

[18] 'Banner of identity': Allievi, S., (2006) 'The shifting significance of the *halal/haram* frontier: Narratives on the *hijab* and other issues', in van Nieuwkerk, K., (ed.) (2006), *Woman Embracing Islam: Gender and Conversion in the West*, University of Texas Press, Austin, Texas, p.132.

[19] Ibid.

[20] Ibid.

[21] Lings, M., (2005) '*A Return to the Spirit: Questions and Answers*', Fons Vitae, USA.

[22] Franks, M., (2000) 'Crossing the borders of whiteness?' 'White Muslim women who wear the *hijab* in Britain today' in *Ethnic and Racial Studies* 23(5), pp. 917-929. Franks views the headscarf as 'neither liberating nor oppressive', and that the power with which it is associated is situated not only in the meaning with which it is invested but also in the circumstances under which it is worn.'

[23] Franks, M., (2000) 'Crossing the borders of whiteness? White Muslim women who wear the *hijab* in Britain today' in *Ethnic and Racial Studies* 23(5), pp. 917-929.

[24] Participants considered that if a prominent fashion designer were to decide that a headscarf is a fashion accessory, women from all walks of life would soon be wearing one.

[25] There have been examples of women denied promotion in employment due to wearing a headscarf. See Allievi, S., (2006) 'The shifting significance of the halal/haram frontier: Narratives on the hijab and other issues,'pp.138-9 in van Nieuwkerk, K., (Ed) (2006) *Women embracing Islam: Gender and Conversion in the West*, University of Texas Press, Austin, Texas. For a variety of perspectives surrounding issues arising in employment from wearing a headscarf, see Jawad, H., (2006) 'Female Conversion to Islam: The Sufi Paradigm' p156, in van Nieuwkerk, K., (Ed) (2006) *Women embracing Islam: Gender and Conversion in the West*, University of Texas Press, Austin, Texas.

[26] For further commentary on racism faced by African-Caribbean heritage converts to Islam see al-Qwidi, M., (2002) 'Understanding the Stages of Conversion: The Voices of British Converts', PhD Thesis, University of Leeds; also see Reddie, R., (2009) *Black Muslims in Britain: Why a Growing Number of Young Black People are Converting to Islam?*' Lion Hudson, Oxford, and Adnan, A., (1999) *New Muslims in Britain*, Ta Ha, London

[27] Allievi (2006).

[28] Allievi (2006).

[29] This view is challenged by some scholars; for example, it is reported by a minority of Muslims scholars that it is permissible for Muslim women to marry non-Muslim men when there is a shortage of suitable potential suitors.

[30] Brice (2011). These two terms are not mutually exclusive; converts can oscillate between the two stages at various points of their conversion.

[31] Some participants believe that ideas are prevalent amongst non-Muslims and in the mass media that women convert to Islam for marriage purposes, or to increase the bonds of attachment within marriages involving Muslim men. According to this mode of thought, women converts are perceived as malleable, whereby their opinions and personalities can be moulded to reflect those of their husbands.

[32] See Rick Banks, an African-American Harvard Professor, who suggests that black women need to consider non-black partners for marriage. Banks, R.R., (2011) *Is marriage for white people? How the African American marriage decline affects everyone,* Penguin Group (USA) Incorporated. See also Banks, S., 'Black woman, white man: should race matter in love? LAtimes.com/news/local/la-me-1008-banks-20111008,0,6813163.column (accessed 25.10.2011)

[33] This discussion was interesting and ran contrary to observations made by Richard Reddie who has argued that African-Caribbean men become more desirable as marriage partners following conversion because of the effects that practising Islam has on their character, making them law abiding, hardworking and committed to their wives and children. See Chapter 8 in Reddie (2009).

[34] See Roald, A.S., (2004) *New Muslims in the European Context: The Experiences of Scandinavians Converts,* p. 99 Koninklijke Brill NV, Leiden. Roald notes that conversion appears to unfold in three phases: firstly, the falling in love stage where the convert is totally absorbed with Islam to the exclusion of all else; the second stage, involving a sense of 'disillusionment' in which heritage Muslims fail to live up to the ideals the convert assumes they should be adhering to; and the third stage, one of 'maturity', where the convert returns to the person they originally were, and incorporates their cultural identity into an Islamic framework.

[35] New converts to Islam are often encouraged to consider marriage proposals on the grounds of a *hadith* which states that the Prophet said that 'marriage is half of faith and those who refrain from it are not from me'. Converts are frequently informed that it is more Islamic not to delay marriage and to respond to proposals of marriage quickly.

[36] Many educated heritage Muslim women assert that it is becoming increasingly problematic to find suitable husbands, as the ratio of educated Muslim males to Muslim females declines, and educated women delay looking for husbands until they have completed their education or established a career.

[37] Arabic – *Subhana Allah* means 'glory to God', and *Allahu Akbar* means 'God is great'; these are used here as expressions of joy.

[38] Arabic – *Astaghfir Allah* means 'seek God's forgiveness', used here to express 'distaste'.

[39] Hindi and Indo-Aryan – '*Gora*' means a 'light skinned person, usually white.'

[40] Arabic – '*kafir*' from the verb '*kafara*' 'to cover or hide,' commonly carries a pejorative meaning.

[41] The *hadith* are religious maxims or aphorisms attributed to the Prophet Muhammad, transmitted orally and collated as a textual body of knowledge in the 8th and 9th Centuries.

[42] For a media discussion of the prevalence of internet pornography in Pakistan, see http://www.foxnews.com/world/2010/07/12/data-shows-pakistan-googling-pornographic-material/

[43] There is a widely reported *hadith* which states that to backbite is considered more reprehensible than committing adultery, because adultery can be forgiven by God, whereas backbiting also requires the forgiveness of the person who was spoken about unfavourably. The strength (validity) of this *hadith* is disputed.

[44] 'If you fear that you shall not be able to deal justly with the orphans, marry women of your choice, two, three or four, but if you fear that you shall not be able to deal justly with them, then only one … that will be more suitable, to prevent you from doing injustice'. Qur'an (4:3)

[45] Part of a *hadith* narrated by Bukhari (vol.7, book 62, *hadith* no. 4887).

[46] Cited in 'Marriages without borders,' Kimberly Merchant www.uiowa.edu/-co19225/marriage1.html

[47] Retaining faith following the collapse of marriage is frequently difficult for women who have had bad experiences of marriage with Muslim men and are unable to disentangle their perceptions of Islam from their husband's behaviour towards them.

[48] See Qur'an (49:12).

[49] There has been little scholarly work done in this area. Some Muslim scholars have written about the division of gender in Islam into four groups: male, female, hermaphrodites (*khuntha*) and *mukhannath*. Khuntha are biological males who identify as female and want to change their biological sex. *Mukhannath* are biological males who (would like to) assume a female gender role but do not want to change their biological sex. The terms *khuntha* and *mukhannath* are not mentioned in the Qur'an. See Yik Koon Teh., 'MakNyahs (Male Transsexuals) in Malaysia: The influence of culture and religion on their identity,' *The International Journal of Transgenderism* Vol.5 No.3, 2001.

[50] The Pakistan Supreme Court in 2011 reported that they would allow a third gender category on the national identity card following successful lobbying by transgendered people. See, 'Pakistan transgenders pin hopes on new rights,' BBC News, 25th April 2011 www.bbc.co.uk/news/world-south-asia-13186958 accessed 27/02/2012.

[51] *Yinyang* is the Taoist concept of opposing dualities forming one balanced whole.

[52] See Leon Moosavi (2011) 'Muslim Converts and Islamophobia in Britain' in Keskin, T., (ed.) *The Sociology of Islam: Secularisation, Economy and Politics*, Reading: Ithaca Press, 2011.

[53] Sarfraz Mansoor recognised the irony of this situation, 'at a time when British Muslims of Asian extraction are increasingly drinking and engaging in sexual permissiveness, White converts are fleeing into piety'. See 'What we Muslims can learn from converts' in The Guardian, 6 January 2011.

[54] Source '*UK Muslim demographics* '(C-RE8-02527) released by Wikileaks and cited in The Daily Telegraph 04.02.2011.

[55] See Office for National Statistics: 2011 Census www.ons.gov.uk/ons/guide-method/census/2011/index.html also see Alan Travis, '*One in Five Young Prisoners are Muslim, Report Reveals*,' in The Guardian December 7, 2012 www.guardian.co.uk/society/2012/dec/07/young-prisoners-muslim

[56] Sarfraz Mansoor maintains that most converts know far more about Islam than most British Pakistanis, see 'What we Muslims can learn from converts,' in The Guardian, 6 January 2011.

[57] *Hijrah* – the period of history when Prophet Muhammad and his followers migrated from Mecca to Medina in 622 CE.

[58] '*The Search for Common Ground: Muslims, non-Muslims and the UK media*,' A Report Commissioned by the Mayor of London, 2007.

[59] Other interest groups such as the Islamic Human Rights Commission, The Forum against Islamophobia and Racism, Islamophobia-Watch.com and the Association for Muslim Rights monitor Islamophobia in Britain as cited in Moosavi,L., 'Muslim Converts and Islamophobia in Britain,' in Keskin, T., '*The Sociology of Islam: Secularism, Economy and Politics*,' Ithaca Press, Reading, 2011.

[60] See Sarfraz Mansoor , 'What we Muslims can learn from converts' The Guardian 6 January 2011.

[61] One participant commented that the 'lack of attention paid to Black converts stems more from the fact that Black women are already seen as Other, therefore, their conversion to something inherently Other such as Islam is less aberrant, and therefore less newsworthy, as when the choice is made by White middle class women.'

[62] See the 1997 Report by the Runnymede Trust, *Islamophobia: A Challenge for Us All*.

[63] See Daily Mail 19 September 2010, 'Britain goes halal…but no one tells the public: How famous institutions serve ritually slaughtered meat with no warning,' by Simon McGee and Martin Delgardo.

[64] See Werbner,P., (2000) 'Divided Loyalties, Empowered Citizenship? Muslims in Britain,' in *Citizenship Studies*, Vol.4, No. 3.

[65] 'Since the genesis of Islam, awareness of Muslims in Europe has been negatively tinged.' See Tahir Abbas, (2005) 'British South Asian Muslims: Before and After September 11[th,]' in Abbas, T.,(2005) (Ed) *Muslim Britain: Communities Under Pressure*, Zed Books, London.

[66] Online YouGov Poll June 2010; see also Haroon Siddique 'Three-quarters of non-Muslims believe Islam negative for Britain,' The Guardian, 2nd August 2010.

[67] See a report by Richard Peppiatt, 'Women & Islam: the rise and rise of the convert,' *The Independent* on Sunday, 06 November 2011. See also Brice, M.A.K., (2010) *A Minority within a Minority: A report on converts to Islam in the United Kingdom*, on behalf of Faith Matters.

[68] Hadith reported by Muslim.

[69] Kenan Malik has accused Muslims of attempting to stifle discourse surrounding Islam and of trying to elicit sympathy and political concessions through exaggerating the existence of Islamophobia. See Malik, K., (2005). 'Islamophobia Myth.' www.kenanmalik.com/essays/prospect_Islamophobia.html (accessed 16.02.2011).

[70] It was reported that post 9/11 sales of the Qur'an soared.

[71] See Geaves, R., (2010) *Islam in Victorian Britain: The Life and Times of Abdullah Quilliam*, Kube Publishing, Markfield.

[72] See Abdul Haqq Baker, 'Repairing the Cracked Lens: Redefining British Muslim Identity in Conservative Britain,' *Journal of Terrorism Research*, Vol.2 Issue 1(2011) www.ojs.st-andrews.ac.uk/index.php/jtr/article/view/177/182 (accessed 07/03/2012).

[73] See Mehdi Hassan, 'How the fear of being criminalised has forced Muslims into silence,' *The Guardian* 8 September, 2011.

[74] 'Inspired by Muhammad,' at www.inspiredbymuhamad.com/

[75] Many *Salafist* adherents maintain that there is no direct link between their interpretation of Islam and radical and extreme ideas, arguing instead that Sufism can appear in extreme and radical guises. See Abdul Haqq Baker's PhD thesis, 'Countering Terrorism in the UK: A convert community perspective', University of Exeter 2009.

[76] Sufi *tariqa*s are Islamic orders following a spiritually infused interpretation of Islam.

[77] *Bay'a* – an Arabic term which refers to the swearing of an oath of allegiance to a particular spiritual guide.

[78] *Dhikr* – remembrance of God – this frequently involves repetitive recitation of the attributes of God.

[79] *Tariqa* Arabic 'way, path or method.' It denotes a Sufi order.

[80] *Barelvi* a movement from the Indian sub-continent supporting traditionalist Islamic beliefs

[81] *Pir* from Urdu meaning a Sufi master.

[82] For a detailed exposition on Sufism see Geaves, R., *The Sufis of Britain: an exploration of Muslim identity*, Cardiff Academic Press, Cardiff, 1999.

[83] This may reflect the Islamic concept of '*urf*' denoting an ability to incorporate non-Islamic customs into a particular culture if they do not contradict the spirit of Islam.

[84] *Chishti* a form of Sufism founded in Chisht, Afghanistan about 930 CE; it emphasizes love, tolerance and openness.

[85] *Sunna*, an Arabic concept denoting the example of the Prophet Muhammad in the conduct of his life.

[86] Yahya Birt (2002) 'Building new Madinas in these sceptred isles,' this article first appeared in 'Q News' and can be accessed at www.yahyabirt.com/files/building_newmadinahs_scan_OCR.pdf

[87] The Mahdi is prophesised by some as a spiritual and temporal ruler destined to establish a reign of righteousness throughout the world.

[88] Muslims are more likely to be the recipients of hate attacks involving serious violence than the instigators, see Vikram Dodd 'Media and Politicians 'fuel rise in hate crimes against Muslims,' *The Guardian*, 28 January 2010, www.guardian.co.uk/uk/2010/jan/28/hate-crimes-muslims-media-politicians/ (accessed 12.03.2012). See also a report by University of Exeter's European Muslim Centre (2010) 'Islamophobia and Anti-Muslim Hate Crime: A London Case Study' by Jonathan Githens-Mazer and Robert Lambert. http://centres.exeter.ac.uk/emrc/publications/Islamophobia_and_Anti-Muslim_Hate_Crime.pdf (accessed 11.04.2012). The report establishes a causal relationship between an environment that habitually demonises Islam and Muslims, stoked by media commentators and populist politicians and religiously motivated hate crimes. The report is dedicated to a PhD student Yasir Abdelmouttalib, left seriously brain damaged after being subjected to a violent hate attack whilst on his way to perform Friday prayer wearing Islamic dress. The report also quotes 2006 figures from Europol which cite that only one out of 498 documented terrorist attacks across Europe could be classed as Islamist, the others being committed by non-Muslim White Europeans (p 25).